HUMMING
YOUR WAY TO
HAPPINESS

Healing and meditative sounds and
Overtone singing from around the world

Dr PETER N GALGUT
Ph.D., M.Phil., M.Sc.

HUMMING YOUR WAY TO HAPPINESS

Healing and meditative sounds and
Overtone singing from around the world

Dr PETER N GALGUT
Ph.D., M.Phil., M.Sc.

BOOKS

WINCHESTER UK
NEW YORK USA

Copyright © 2005 O Books
O Books is an imprint of The Bothy, John Hunt Publishing Ltd.,
Deershot Lodge, Park Lane, Ropley, Hants, SO24 0BE, UK
office@johnhunt-publishing.com
www.O-books.net

Distribution in:
UK
Orca Book Services
orders@orcabookservices.co.uk
Tel: 01202 665432 Fax: 01202 666219 Int. code (44)

USA and Canada
NBN
custserv@nbnbooks.com
Tel: 1 800 462 6420 Fax: 1 800 338 4550

Australia
Brumby Books
sales@brumbybooks.com
Tel: 61 3 9761 5535 Fax: 61 3 9761 7095

New Zealand
Peaceful Living
books@peaceful-living.co.nz
Tel: 64 7 57 18105 Fax: 64 7 57 18513

Singapore
STP
davidbuckland@tlp.com.sg
Tel: 65 6276 Fax: 65 6276 7119

South Africa
Alternative Books
altbook@global.co.za
Tel: 27 011 792 7730 Fax: 27 011 972 7787

Text: © Peter N Galgut, 2005

Design: BookDesign™, London

ISBN 1 905047 14 2

A CIP catalogue record for this book is available from the
British Library.

Printed in the USA by Maple-Vail Manufacturing Group

The source of some of these images collected over the internet have been difficult to
trace. Any ommissions on credits will be rectified on the next printing.

CONTENTS

About the author

The author is a medical scientist and clinician at London University, who has had a lifelong interest in alternative therapies and religions. He is a qualified Acupuncturist and a Homeopath, which he applies in addition to his clinical practice, research and teaching.

Introduction

A JOURNEY

IT'S A LONG JOURNEY! It is indeed a very long, long journey! It's a journey that goes to many places and through many places. Many of the paths lead to dead ends. And many of the paths end up as circles ... ending where they started!

But what is this long journey?

Really, it's quite difficult to explain, it's difficult to describe, and it's even difficult to share with others! It's a very personal and individual journey and each person, only as an individual, can travel it. We all have many journeys to travel in life, and for each one of us they are different! Yes, we are all born, and go to school, and grow up, and learn to make a living, and earn our daily bread and hopefully reach a middle-age, and then old-age, and then fade into oblivion, hopefully without suffering too much along the way. But that is a physical journey that we must all take, with variations on a theme.

There are, of course, other journeys! One of these is a very special journey! A journey less well defined, a journey into the unknown, the journey into the beyond, and beyond the beyond! In some ways it's a journey into ourselves, but in other ways it's a journey out of ourselves. It's a journey that searches for something elusive, though it's always there and yet it isn't! Sometimes a little glimpse out of the corner of your eye and when you look - it's gone; sometimes a strange feeling or sometimes it's simply a need to connect to something. Sometimes a little sound and when you listen - it's gone!

This book is about a journey into sounds and rhythms that may help us to reach out and connect. To help us find ... something! It is, one of many long and frustrating journeys. Sometimes, it seems like they are endless journeys, not only that, but journeys without direction without beginning and without an end. But that's no reason to stop searching, that's no reason to stop trying to find the path, the key to the door of revelation and understanding, and the way forward.

Like so many others, I have tried different ways to capture that glimpse, that feeling, that sound, that little whisper, that rustle of leaves, that quiet whistle of the winds, the sound of stillness when I'm alone ... the sounds of nature breathing!

But we have to start our journey somewhere and so what better place to start than religion. Most of us were brought up to believe in the religion of our parents, or our communities or our society in general. Many of us simply absorbed the culture that surrounds us, which is often based on the beliefs and values of the prevalent religion in a community. And so it was for me, brought up with an image of God and a code of ethics and a set of rules and behavior patterns that somehow or another related to that God. This seemed to be somehow linked to that metaphysical greater reality in our souls and in all that surrounds us. Surely, somewhere, within the highly structured and formalized ritual and religious study lay the grains of true spirituality, of "connectedness", of a sense of inner peace or being in tune with everything. But somehow or other, for all the pomp and ceremony and all the sanctimonious words and inspirational music ... it wasn't there! Well, maybe ... just occasionally ... inspirational and uplifting moments from the music or communal singing, but then ... well, these were usually only fleeting moments ... and always so elusive!

And what of alternative religions? In many ways the alternative religions, the New Age movement, and the move in Western society towards Eastern religions, is a response to that very emptiness and meaningless ritual of formalized Western religions. There are many paths to travel in search of tranquility and peace among the many alternative religions. Unfortunately, it seems as though human nature has a remarkable propensity for reducing the most inspirational concepts to meaningless ritual, and why are we so surprised? It's much easier to dress up in some outlandish dress, brandishing shiny objects and uttering meaningless jargon, than it is to actually explore our inner selves and maybe feel or become aware of that elusive something that so many of us are searching for, and yet cannot describe. And so, many of the alternative religions also turn out to be disappointing! Yet another cult, yet another path, yet another dead end, and the need for yet another change in direction.

The Eastern philosophies seem to offer so much. The concepts of universal peace, of being "in tune" with that universal physical and metaphysical reality that surrounds us and the possibility of achieving some form of heightened awareness, self-actualization, or "enlightenment" are enticing inducements for the searching traveler. The concept of meditation, with the possibility of withdrawing from the physical world, focusing on the metaphysical, and finding the secret doorway to the greater reality, offer such potential! And yes, it's shrouded in mystery and concepts that we don't fully understand, making them even more inviting as our search continues. All you need is a mantra and maybe a mandala (a circular, cosomological painting), and time to concentrate, undisturbed and ... but that's the problem ... undisturbed! Ever tried meditating, thinking hard, concentrating and being very focused, just as the sirens of a passing police car shatter your solace, or the telephone rings, or you're called to do some jobs around the house, or even nature calls? Ever tried meditating in the evening after a hard day's work? What happens? You fall asleep! Yet another wasted journey, and yet another change in direction as the search goes on.

Most of us have to achieve a balance between our personal lives, our professional lives, and the day-to-day routines that make-up our lives and we simply cannot retire to some quiet mountain retreat in the Himalayas. In any case many of the so-called retreats have turned into a cult centers, losing that crucial essence which is subjugated into the personality of one pre-eminent individual. No, it's not there either! Maybe staring into crystals, or bowls of water, or hugging trees or something ... but realistically speaking, for most of us, spending hours at a time staring into a bowl of water or the flame of a candle or whatever, is simply not possible. So the search goes on in amongst the clutter of the daily routines and responsibilities of our lives, always interrupted and always taking second place to more pressing daily responsibilities.

But there must be some way to help us "tune in", or just relax and unwind our minds, however little, without subjugating our souls to the rigors of theological or philosophical fervor? Of all of the sensations flooding into our consciousness all day and every day, sounds play such an important part: the urgency of the police car sirens, the demand for instant attention by the ring of the telephone, the general clatter of life that buzzes endlessly in our ears. But then there are the other sounds ... a crying baby, the whimpering puppy, the sounds of nature, and songs, and music ... that all touch us different ways. Maybe it would help to explore these sounds to try and find that magic sound that could that may open the doors to the blissful peace that we're searching for so desperately.

And so the journey begins ...

THE ORIGINS OF LANGUAGE AND SOUND

COMMUNICATION BY USING language evolved slowly, and three primary sounds emerged fairly universally. The sound "ee" was used for to express this sense of threat, fear or emotional stress. The more relaxed "aah" sound was (and still is) an expression of comfort and satisfaction. The "oo" the sound expressed pain or discomfort of some kind. These letters became the primary vowels. Consonants slowly emerged from the primordial grunts of human communication.

One of the oldest languages to have survived up to today with its traditions intact is Hebrew. The three letters of the Hebrew alphabet forming the foundation of the Kabalistic tree (see later), known as the "mother" letters (Y,H,V,), are associated with physical parts of the body, in descending order, the head, the heart, and the abdomen. These different vowel sounds were used in ancient times to resonate specifically to different parts of the body, and also to manage the emotional tone of the prayers using the resonances of the letters and words themselves. These resonant contemplations were enhanced by the use of chanted melodies. Many references to phrases such as "opening your heart" in the Bible are derived directly from such sonic and harmonic contemplations linking bodily form to harmonic tones. The resonances produced in communal prayer therefore create not only external resonances with the cosmos, but also a communal resonance among those participating, as well as internalized resonances focusing the harmonic vibrations to key areas of the body such as the heart. In this way the physical body, or parts of the physical body might be linked, connected with or tuned into the cosmos, or parts of the cosmos. In the Hebrew prayers (as well as in other ancient religious traditions) therefore, one would expect to find frequent use of the "ah" sound. It should also be noted that the Bible tells us that God "breathed" life into Adam and the sound of exhaling air is "aahh". Therefore this sound resonates directly to God himself. When the "aahh" sound is added to the three mother letters described above in the form of an H, the very name of God (in Hebrew) is produced (Y,H,V,H), emphasizing that crucial importance of sounds and harmonics in Judaism. In the same way, the name of God in Islam, Allah, begins and ends with the very self-same sound.

Of all the grunts and basic sounds used by primitive humans, it was the vowels that provided and gave meaning to the consonants. Letters such "n", "m", "k", are basic sounds but it is the vowels that link these sounds together to give harmonic resonance to words. It is therefore the vowels that form the basis of language, linking of the consonants to form words, giving the words the meaning and even feeling. It is the harmonics generated by the vowels, uttered with the physical body, which may resonate into the spiritual realms. Therefore tuning the vowel sounds particularly is believed to resonate with the different centers of the physical and the spiritual bodies.

Most ancient cultures and primitive peoples regarded sound as a creative, generative force associated with the creation of the Universe, and capable of being harnessed to produce impossible physical and spiritual feats.

Many primitive cultures were aware of the inherent physical qualities of vocal and natural sound. It was considered to be a God-given language.

SACRED SPHERES

THE IDEA THAT sounds can have special mystical powers, or may facilitate communion with ancestral spirits or the ultimate spiritual power in the Universe has many origins that vary between ancient peoples. One of the most sophisticated theories of the magical or sacred qualities of sounds and numbers was developed by the ancient Greeks.

Geometric forms have long fascinated ancient philosophers. Circles, squares, pentagrams/hexagrams and their three-dimensional equivalents of circles, cubes, and polyhedrons have all been given special mystical qualities. While different geometric patterns based on straight lines such as cubes and hexagrams create intriguing inter-relationships, spheres are among the most intriguing of all. Spheres do not have separate sides as do other geometric constructions, but consist essentially of one overall and uniform side. Because, they do not have corners or angles, the mathematical formulae that describe them are totally different to any straight-sided shapes. Not only do they have very special physical and geometric characteristics, but also their interaction with light and sound is unique. Tapping a metal ball will elicit a sound in the same way as any other shaped metal object. The sound is produced by vibrations, (or more correctly, oscillations,) that occur within the structure of the sphere. Physicists such as Horace Lamb (1882) investigated the acoustic oscillations emanating from sonically vibrating spheres and found two distinct types of oscillation. The first type, known as "spheroidal" mode, creates uniform pulsating oscillations throughout the sphere, whereas the second type, known as "torsional" mode, create simultaneous twisting oscillations in opposite directions within the body of the sphere. The actual tone produced by any given sphere depends predominantly on its diameter, as well as its structure and constituents. Therefore, each sphere has a unique fundamental note that can be thought of as its unique natural frequency. Due to the different oscillation effects occurring within acoustically activated spheres, unique harmonic oscillations are produced to create a unique sound picture for that sphere. As the most prominent objects in the Universe appear to be spheres, it seemed obvious that the Universe and it's contents were interlinked by a matrix of harmonic tones or oscillations.

Pythagoras was fascinated by numbers and mathematics in general. He was also was the first person on record to have noticed the relationship between tones produced and the size of objects from which they emanate. He was the first person to attempt to integrate the progression of tones and their harmonics, with mathematical number progressions. The relationship between numbers and musical notes appeared to him to represent manifestations of divine resonances. He believed that the centre of order, beauty and harmony in the cosmos was governed by three fixed notes in the ratio of 1:2, 2:3, and 3:4. Order arising from chaos, centered on these three notes was believed to generate universal "harmony". The three fixed musical intervals of the octave, the 4th, and 5th were considered to be fixed primary sounds from which balance and universal harmony emanated. These primal number ratios were therefore considered to be responsible for the harmony emanating from the divine. They therefore governed the structure and balance in the world, and the spheres (i.e. the orbs) that encircle it. Mathematics therefore had not only a mechanical purpose, but was divinely inspired as part of the spiritual or metaphysical parts of creation.

The Pythagorean school extended their concept of divine reverberations into astronomy in an attempt to understand the apparently mechanical clockwork cycles of the earthly seasons, and movements of the heavenly bodies. In their view, the whole of creation could be described and understood in terms of numbers and pure musical tones. Pythagoras believed that all of creation evolved from pure tonal vibrations. These musical tones could not be heard as they were beyond the normal hearing range. Large bodies such as the Earth have such deep and ponderous natural vibrations that it is impossible to hear or sense them directly. Similarly, all of creation and particularly the prominent heavenly bodies such as the sun and the moon and the planets, were considered to be interconnected and controlled by these sounds that came to be called "The Music of the Spheres". Essentially this meant that the whole of the Universe was constructed according to a musical scale. The Greek word harmonium literally means "connected together", and cosmos (spelt in Greek *kosmos*) means "the beautiful order of things".

Later, Greek philosophers attempted to equate the major heavenly bodies with musical scales. For example if the Earth was resonating at the fundamental note, then the closest body (i.e. the moon) would represent the first harmonic with the shortest interval, while Saturn being the most distant heavenly body, would represent the highest, or most distant, harmonic from the fundamental. Having integrated the tones and their harmonics into musical scales of the heavenly bodies it was then a small perceptual step to see the Universe as an harmonious musical and numerical entity. Thus was born the concept of "sacred spheres". Many variations in concepts of the sacred spheres have evolved over the following centuries. Some mathematicians and philosophers tried to correlate the diameters of the different heavenly bodies to different musical tones and scales, while others related the distance of these heavenly bodies from the earth to musical scales.

Astronomers such as William Herschel were also accomplished musicians and composers. Several of his musical compositions survive, inspired by his astronomical observations. More recently (1930), Gustav Holtz composed *The Planets* Suite. In this composition he gave tonal qualities to each planet. The tone and musical picture for each planet was inspired by their mythological and astrological qualities from the ancient Greeks, as well as their appearance from the earth. The underlying inspiration was the concept that as these spheres spun around their axes and in their orbits around the sun, they would create a hum or drone in tune with their physical size movement and position.

The humming, pulsating or oscillating nature of all matter is even today a matter of great scientific debate. Heavenly bodies such as pulsars are so named because of the pulsating bursts of radiation generated as they rotate. At the other end of the scale, atomic physics has found not only specific oscillation pictures for each element in nature, but even the atomic sub-particles are in a state of constant vibration across a wide spectrum of frequencies. The oscillations, rotations and interactions between these particles are not unlike the mathematical equivalent of the timbre produced by complex musical instruments such as the violin. As these never-ending physical oscillations are perpetuated throughout the Universe, from the smallest sub-particles to the greatest concentrations of matter in the Universe, so they produce radiations of electromagnetic energy such as light, X-rays, and radio waves. In the same way as music is created by oscillations introduced into physical matter, these infinite and harmoniously integrated oscillations throughout the whole spectrum of nature must have musical qualities. As each sub-particle, particle or body in the Universe has a characteristic electromagnetic radiation, so too must be every part of the Universe have a specific sound, or a musical and harmonic characteristic. This music cannot be heard because music requires a medium for transmission. On Earth this is air, but in space, consisting of a vacuum, there is no audible sound as we know it.

Nevertheless, the Holistic, the New Age Movement, alternative religions, and many ancient religions and traditions have tried to "tune in" to these "sacred sounds". Attempting to produce them in an audible form by drumming, singing, dancing, and in some way tuning in and harmonizing with them is a characteristic found in most cultures. In particular, the intonation of specific vowels, words, mantras, or Overtone singing techniques attempt to set up personal vibratory eminences, which it is hoped could harmonize, and amplify the primary oscillations of creation. While on a personal level trying to harmonize with the natural vibrations of nature by using sounds and harmonies can be a deep and profound internal journey towards health and happiness, there are those who have sought far more profound external journeys. Using the most prominent heavenly bodies that are visible from Earth and particularly focusing on their ancient mystical qualities has been the source of profound spiritual development for many. As these heavenly bodies (or spheres or orbs) are part of creation, and vibrate in harmony with it, the concept of "sacred spheres" has evolved both in music and in spiritual development.

THE MUSIC OF THE SPHERES

THE THEOLOGY AND philosophy in medieval Europe centered on order and harmony in the Universe. This reached its zenith in Victorian times when order and harmony in relationships, family life, community life, national and international relationships took precedence over all else. Philosophers, astronomers, and mathematicians tried hard to calculate the laws governing planetary motion, cosmic order and harmony often based on the ancient Greek theories. Considerable scientific endeavor was also spent on trying to reduce social behavior to numerical formulae. The science of numerology grew to pre-eminence following on Pythagoras' assertion that the entire Universe was derived from and ruled by numbers, sacred sounds and harmonies.

Central to the numbers and mathematical formulations, was the influence of music with its tempos and harmonies, which were believed to be the unifying factor. In many ancient cultures music was considered to be a direct expression of the Divine, and its harmonies an emanation of the core energy of the Universe itself. The astronomer Johannes Kepler (1571-1630) related most of his work on planetary movements and angles to music. Rene Descartes (1596-1650) considered that the sounds, rhythms, and tunes of music could be reduced to simple mathematical formulations, while Leibniz (1646-1716) considered music to be a conscious manifestation of numerical progressions. These philosophers and scientists perpetuated the Pythagorean tradition that all of creation is simply a matter of sounds interacting in harmony, and expressed in numbers.

While the ancient Greeks developed many different musical scales, these grew more sophisticated with time and experimentation. In medieval times the musical scale from which almost all Western music is founded was standardized as a seven-note scale. At this time the most outlying planets in our solar system (Pluto and Uranus) had not been discovered, and so there were only seven visible planets. The seven-note musical scale is not coincidental, as each note was said to represent each planet. Each planet had its characteristic tone and harmonies and its mystical attributes. As each heavenly sphere had its characteristic sound signature, it also moved through the heavens in its own characteristic way. As a result, sacred dancing was adopted in many religious sects. Singing, to harmonize with the spheres, and dancing to reproduce the orderly progress of heavenly spheres has formed the cornerstone of much religious expression. By reproducing the harmony of heavens both physically and harmonically on earth, the harmony of the Universe is believed to be amplified in the participants.

TURNING EAST

UNFORTUNATELY, WITH INCREASING sophistication in our knowledge of music it has been found that the mathematical intervals described initially by Pythagoras, and standardized in our musical traditions in the West have been found to be invalid. The mathematical proportions of notes in a musical scale in harmony with the fundamental note have been found to be not in the exact mathematical proportions than they were originally thought to be. Rather than accepting these nuances in nature, the scales were "tempered" so as to conform to the Pythagorean mathematical relationships, making them slightly out of tune. By definition therefore, much of our musical tradition in the West is "out of tune" with nature. While our ears have become accustomed to music produced by these slightly out of tune harmonies, and we can be stimulated emotionally and sometimes physically, or obtain states of uplifting spirituality by engaging with Western music, there are many who feel that to retune to the harmonies inherent in nature, we need to turn to the more primitive forms of music and the primordial sounds of nature.

The musical scales of the world are derived from the harmonic relationships between the Overtones generated by musical notes. A form of annotation of musical values developed over time leading to the current musical annotation system. As the Pythagorean School believed that the scales were based on a strict mathematical progression, this was reproduced in the musical annotation. The major disadvantage of this musical annotation system is that the notes represent specific intervals between each vibration frequency. It is therefore impossible to even consider the possibility of intermediate frequencies between each integral step. As a result Western music is based on a progression of fixed mathematical proportions, which exclude intermediate fractions of a frequency step. In Asian and other Eastern cultures, music and singing can be intoned in "fractions" of the tone to create richer and unusual harmonies.

It is also for this reason that the music of the ancient traditions initially sounds distinctly unmusical and out of tune to the Western ear. Tibetan chanting, the Hindu Ragas, Balanes, Gamalon and other singing or chanting traditions can actually sound so discordant as to be unnerving to the Western ear. The buzzing of the fundamental note which is often set at such a low frequency as to sound like a deep throated cough or rumble may even sound inhuman or animalistic to the uninitiated. However, from these deep-seated growls and grunts, spontaneous whistling harmonies arise more readily than from fundamental notes that have been "tempered" for Western musical traditions.

Similarly using only simple musical instruments such as gongs, bells, chimes, musical bowls, the didgeridoo and similar simple instruments should only be used to produce pure sounds. Overtone singing, as practiced in Tuva and the surrounding regions, like the musical traditions of other ancient peoples, produce a range of harmonics in tune with nature, rather than in tune with Western traditions. "Non tempered" music is said to spontaneously produce harmonics or Overtones from droning or humming fundamental notes that are more in tune with the ethereal vibrations of Nature.

Nevertheless, this does not negate the value of Western song and music. The Pythagorean scale reproduced on a piano working from left to right across the keyboard forms a continuous repeating spiral of musical harmonies rising to ever-higher pitches with each cycle. The concept of a circular rising and repeating spiral of notes in harmony, spiraling into infinity has profound psychological, theological, and even scientific importance. The generation of an infinite spiral of harmonious Overtones, tuning in to the infinite, or focusing on the natural harmonies of the world around us, or the orbs of the heavens, or even the building blocks of matter itself may be the key to unlocking the door to the great powers and influences that surround us. Tuning into the right harmonies and so stimulating the right emotional or psychological states using music, may form the bridge between the physical and spiritual aspects of human existence.

But before we can fully understand the theory of music the nature of ancient sacred sounds, we need to explore the way in which harmony has evolved in Western culture. And so our journey sounds and harmonies continues.

'1'

A short history of Western music composition and harmonic theory

HARMONIC THEORY IS credited to Pythagoras who was passing a metal foundry. As he passed, he became aware of the beating of the hammers on the metal being shaped. He observed that the hammers of each worker made a different sound.

PYTACORA

As the hammers were of constant size and shape, he wondered if the different shapes of the object being made did not create the different sounds. He set about experimenting with different shapes and sizes of metallic objects such as bells, and different lengths of twine. He hung the hammers on strings, and then plucked the strings and noted that the strings produced different notes when the hammers were hung in different positions. In the process, Pythagoras created the laws of harmonics based on mathematical relationships between notes in harmony. By observing the geometric differences between notes, for example changing the length of the taught twine while a note was being sounded, subsidiary notes (i.e. harmonic or Overtone notes, which we now call "partials",) were produced that vibrated in harmony with the base or fundamental note of the full length string. In his experiments, Pythagoras, produced the fundamental note by vibrating the whole length of the string. The first Overtone (the octave) was produced by dividing the string in half, the next Overtone (the fifth) by dividing the string into thirds, and the next Overtone (the fourth) by dividing the string into quarters and so on. This mathematical progression is known as an harmonic scale in music. These laws of harmony form the basis of Western music composition.

Therefore, the principles of harmonic vibrations (or oscillations) are based on the following primary proportions: -

2:1 is an octave (example 880/440 vibrations/second)
3:2 is a 5th   (example 660/440 vibrations/second)
4:3 is a 4th   (example 585/440 vibrations/second)

Pythagoras attempted to integrate music with mathematics, because he believed that these numbers were the basis for all natural systems. He believed that these were the numbers to which the Universe vibrated in harmony, and later this became almost synonymous with the "lost chord". The assumption was that if this universal vibration of the Universe could be harnessed, and amplified, hugely powerful forces would be released. Such stories as the destruction of the walls of Jericho by means of sounding of specific notes on trumpets are based on the use of this special chord.

A string that vibrates along its entire length at a frequency of 440 vibrations per second will produce the note A, above middle C. This is the standard note to which concert orchestras are tuned, and it is therefore known as "concert pitch". It will vibrate at twice that speed if its length is halved, producing an A note one octave higher, and three times that speed when divided into thirds, sounding the high E that is five notes above the second A note. A series can be built up in this way, known as an Overtone series. The first eight notes of the series form an octave, which forms the basis of the musical scales in common usage. This led to a development of a full harmonic system itself, which was considered by early Greek philosophers to represent "natural acoustics". As a result, theories were developed, based on the "harmony of this spheres" describing the movement of the planet's through space.

The musical ratio of 2:1 represents an octave. If the fundamental note is A, its frequency, (or oscillations) is 440 times per second. The note eight tones higher in a musical scale, forms the octave, and it will oscillate at exactly double the rate, (ie 880 times per second). Similarly the ratio of 3: 2 represents an interval called a 5th. It is the 5th note on a scale, and on the scale of A, it is an E, which oscillates at a frequency of 660 oscillations per second. The interval of a 4th, representing the ratio of 4: 3, on the scale of A is a D, and a 3rd will be C#. The intervals of one, two, three and four were considered by Pythagoras to form a sacred sequence known as the *tetraktys* (meaning "the fours). When these numbers are added up the sum is ten and when arrayed into a triangle with four at the bottom and one at that top, they form a perfect triangle, which was thought to have deep mystical significance.

The word scale is derived from the Italian word *scala*, meaning a ladder. Many scales have evolved, but these have been standardized in the West by dividing the octave into twelve discreet units, called notes. A complete scale of twelve notes is known as a chromatic scale. The set of notes are made up of a combination of some full steps and some half steps to give an overall scale of eight intervals containing twelve notes.

The most basic Western scale is made up of the first two Overtones: - the octave and the 5th. By 'geometric progression' twelve of these fifths creates a full musical scale that is slightly over seven octaves (the extra bit being known as a 'Pythagorean coma'). If these twelve tones are reduced to fit into a single octave, we create a classical twelve-note octave scale on which all musical composition in the West is based. To improve the quality of the harmony between the notes, in music composition, the intervals between the notes have been equalized, so that they are no longer quite in tune with those arising spontaneously in nature. Some recent composers have attempted to use unequalized harmonies in their compositions to achieve unusual effects.

Several sub-scales have also evolved with time. The most popular sub-scale is the major scale. This scale evolved from the time of Pythagoras and subsequently, when people discovered that the octave and the 5th interval sounded pleasing. The 5th falls halfway in the octave on the frequency scale. When rising up or descending a scale (of 8 notes), the 4th note is at the halfway mark. The 4th is therefore the inverse or reciprocal of the 5th. Essentially the scale was subdivided into the 4th, the 5th, contained in the octave (3/4, 2/3 & 1/2). If a vibrating string produces C, it will sound an F at three-quarters of its length, and a G at two thirds of its length, and an octave at half its length giving the essential scale of the base note, the 4th, the 5th, and the octave. The 2nd and the 6th notes were added later to form the major scale as we know it.

Pitch	A	A	E	A	C#	E	G	A
Frequency	110	220	330	440	550	660	770	880
Harmonic	1	2	3	4	5	6	7	8

STAVE MUSIC

The human voice produces Overtones from a single fundamental note, and follows the laws of harmonics. In musical terms, a basic fundamental note (in the form of a hum or drone) produces an harmonic scale that includes the notes of an octave, fifth, fourth, a series of thirds, followed by a series of seconds.

Each of our voices (even while speaking) produces a range of Overtones (i.e. harmonics) simultaneously. The skill of the Overtone singer lies in being able to focus on specific Overtones and to amplify them so that they can be distinctly heard.

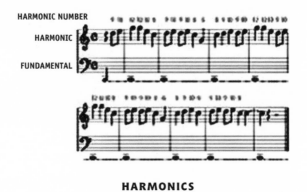

HARMONICS

An harmonic is a musical note that is part of an ascending series of notes that that are in harmony with a basic (i.e. fundamental) pitch. Sound is made up of a number of different notes (representing different frequencies of sound) that combine to form different sounds. The **pitch** is the note at the start, or the base of the series of notes, and it is also called the **fundamental**. The frequencies of the notes that sound above the fundamental are harmonically related to the fundamental, are called **scales**. The characteristic sound of a combination of notes in a scale or combination of scales is called the **spectrum** of a sound. The sound spectrum gives rise to the **timbre** or texture of a sound. A good example of timbre is listening to the same note played by different instruments, for example a flute and a violin. The violin produces a richer or fuller note, which is completely different to the pure and clear whistle-like note of a flute, even though these two instruments play the same note.

THE HARMONIC SPECTRUM

THE DIFFERENT NOTES in a musical scale are sounded at different frequencies to form an **harmonic spectrum**. The notes making up these series are known as **Overtones** or **partials**. When the series of notes complement each other to form a pleasing sound they are in **harmony**, which means that they are in tune with each other. If the notes are out of tune, they clash with each other to give a grating, or unpleasant sound, producing an **inharmonic spectrum**. This is also called **dissonance**.

Harmonic frequencies are exact whole-number multiples of the fundamental: The first harmonic ($1 \times 1 = 1$) is the fundamental or base note; the second harmonic ($1 \times 2 = 2$) sounds at twice the frequency of the fundamental; the third harmonic sounds at three times the frequency of the fundamental, and so on. The diagram below breaks down a harmonic spectrum of a sound with five harmonics. The combination of all the harmonics is shown at the bottom of the diagram below. The sounds you will hear are in the graphic form of sine waves. Sine waves graphically illustrate pure sounds without any harmonic Overtones. A single harmonic is simply a sine wave of a single specific sound at a specific frequency. It represents graphically a string vibrating to produce the sound as used in Pythagoras' experiments. What makes an harmonic distinctive to a given instrument is the presence of specific harmonics characteristic of the instrument. What makes the harmonic distinctive is its role in producing the sensation on the part of the listener of the emitting instrument's tone quality.

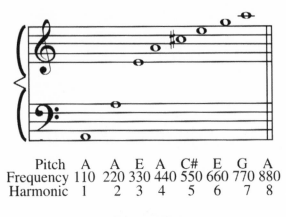

Pitch	A	A	E	A	C#	E	G	A
Frequency	110	220	330	440	550	660	770	880
Harmonic	1	2	3	4	5	6	7	8

STAVE MUSIC

The harmonic spectrum of a musical instrument is the unique and characteristic sound that it makes when a note is sounded. In the example above, the same note on a violin and a flute are indeed the same note, but they sound different. The richness of the sound of a violin is because the note being played (i.e. the fundamental) sets off a wider range of subsidiary notes (i.e. partials, harmonics or Overtones) than a flute. This sounds like a fuller, or richer, but less pure, sound than when the same note is sounded on a flute. More correctly, the harmonic spectrum of the violin is greater than that of a flute. This occurs because each instrument, due to its design, the materials from which it is made and its method of producing notes, amplifies certain harmonic notes and suppresses others. These partials, or Overtones make up the unique harmonic spectrum that produces the characteristic timbre of each instrument or sound.

MUSIC AND OVERTONE SINGING

SOUND IS PRODUCED by waves of air pressure acting on our eardrums. In speech and song the waves are set in motion when the vocal cords of the larynx open and close in a rhythmic fashion. The flow of air out of the lungs causes the air pressure to vibrate at a fundamental frequency, or pitch. This is not usually pure sound as it also contains a mixture of harmonics, above the fundamental pitch. The lowest fundamental that is achievable in the West is a low C note whose frequency is 65.4 hertz; its harmonics are 130.8 hertz, 196.2 hertz and so on. The strength of the harmonics diminishes as their frequencies rise, making them progressively less audible, until they become completely inaudible.

Because the windpipe is a tube through which the sound travels, it has the acoustical property of being able to resonate in harmony with a fundamental note sounded when air passes through it. The specific and characteristic audible Overtones of different sound producing instruments (including the vocal chords, throat etc.) are called "formants". In the mouth, they are created by the resonance of the sound created in the vocal cords. As the sound wave leaves the mouth, it loses energy, which we recognise as getting softer. In effect, as it gets softer, the lower frequencies are dampened to a greater extent than the higher frequencies. As a result, the harmonics decrease in power except for peaks, which are the formants. These occur at specific frequencies for each sound-producing instrument depending on its resonance characteristics. As everybody has a slightly different length, size and shape of their windpipes, vocal cords, mouths and lips, their voices all sound different. This is because resonance causes some notes to be amplified or dampened in a way that gives each voice its unique sound.

Throat singing and other kinds of Overtone singing enable a singer to create more than one audible note at the same time. Altering the shape of the mouth and throat, using different organs for producing the fundamental sound such as the vocal chords or chest, and altering the flow of breath through the mouth and nose achieve this. By performing these changes while singing, different resonating spaces, are created creating harmonic Overtones that are of a different note from the fundamental being sounded. The effect is likened to the sound of bagpipes which produce an underlying drone or hum (i.e. the fundamental), over which the melody is produced using a separate and specifically calibrated pipe to produce the notes that are in harmony with the fundamental base note.

Mastering Overtone singing techniques takes considerable practice and exercise. Many practitioners describe how creating the Overtones engenders a profound sense of inner awareness and peace. Often this results in a heightened awareness of metaphysical aspects of human existence, and this is said to cause adepts at these techniques to be transported beyond their physical planes of existence.

MUSIC AND MEDITATION

IN MOST ANCIENT traditions, whether Tibetan Buddhism, Hinduism, Judaism, Christianity, or shamanism (whether Mongolian/ Tuvinian, Aboriginal, African, or Native American Indian,) the sounding of divine names and sacred resonances are used as the foundation for many rituals to invoke and solicit the help of the divine. Often this is combined with visualization techniques to concentrate the invocation of the divine and other spiritual energies. The sounds are usually at a very low and hollow pitch, slowly reverberating with repetitive rhythms that are almost hypnotic in character. If the right frequency and rhythm can be established and sustained, the phenomenon termed by some as "entrainment" occurs. In this state, the fundamental and its Overtones harmonize with the natural basic brain waves. The brain has natural oscillating frequencies of between 4 and 12 Hz. The natural reverberating frequency of the Earth is said to be 7.83 Hz. It is therefore at these very low and slow frequencies that one is potentially able to tune in to the most fundamental and profound frequencies of nature and planet Earth itself. By sounding or chanting at these frequencies, the performer is able to harmonize the frequencies of the Earth with their own brains, resulting in profound spiritual experiences. However, most people are not able to spend the time and effort in developing the ability to chant at these low frequencies and elicit the magical Overtones from such techniques as Tuvinian throat singing, or Tibetan chanting. Actively listening to and engaging with the chants of a proficient practitioner may enable us to harmonize our brains with that of the performer, drawing us towards these self-same frequencies, helping to bring us into tune with our world.

But these are not the only pure sounds of nature surrounding us that we can tune into and visualize. The sounds and sight of the ocean, the whistling wind, the rustling of branches in the forest, chirping of birds, the rumbling of distant thunder, and so many sounds of nature, may promote in us a sense of natural peace and calmness.

One of our most important and fundamental natural rhythms is our heartbeat and rhythms of our breathing. Many ancient traditions, particularly the Native Americans have centered their sacred sounds on these natural body rhythms. Reproducing the heartbeat, or concentrating breathing rhythms by repetitive drumming or activities such as dancing, have a profound effect in creating states of altered perception and spiritual peace. These techniques are often easier to perform than Overtone singing and chanting techniques of the East, and so are easier for non adepts to practice and participate in. Nevertheless, an adept person, whether a shaman, witch doctor, medicine man, or tribal chief, is usually needed to guide and facilitate the attainment of these trance-like states in participants. In some cases such as the Gospel churches found in many parts of the USA and elsewhere, and the whirling dervishes, these trance states may be amplified to such an extent by repetitive practice that they may lead to loss of control, or physical collapse. In such states, normal conscious perception recedes, and in the altered state of religious fervor, participants may experience visions, release of emotional and physical tension, and realize altered perceptions of their physical, psychological or spiritual lives.

Different parts of the brain have different functions. Some parts of the brain are devoted to the five physical senses of sight, hearing, taste, touch, and smell. Other parts of our brains are devoted to emotions, temperament, dreams and subconscious fantasies and feelings. It is thought that chanting or humming, or carrying out repetitive movements for extended periods of time can stimulate those parts of the brain devoted to feelings and emotions, as opposed to those parts devoted to the sensory world with which we interact continuously. In stimulating this part of the brain, not only can we promote feelings of peace and changes in our moods and our outlook on life, but we may also be able to transcend our everyday existence, rise above ourselves and the frustrations of our lives and maybe even begin spiritual journeys beyond our consciousness, or even farther afield, to discover parts of ourselves that we never knew existed and to which we had no access before.

CIRCLES AND SPIRALS

IN MANY CULTURES in which music is either produced by chanting or intoning of sacred symbols, or the use of musical instruments, communal singing, and dancing, these rituals are performed in a circle. The importance of the circle cannot be underestimated. In Western formal music, the structure is considered to be linear. In a typical concerto there would be three or four sections. As the orchestra, solo instrument or choir progresses through each section, the music changes from an introductory passage to a climax and then an ending. In most of the sacred music of chanting, Overtone singing, and the intonation of sacred sounds, the structure of the music is circular. It doesn't progress through a set step like progression, but it goes round and round in a repetitive way returning each time to the beginning and following the same course as before. This repetitive and often enhanced rhythmic cycling of sacred sounds, creates a harmony with the natural rhythms of the body and mind resulting in states of altered perception. These states are achieved and nurtured in the sacred rituals of many communities throughout the world.

But the circle has many more fundamental functions! Underlying all of the physical aspects of the circle is the concept that it represents completeness, the cycle of life, and of creation itself. First, and most important is that all participants face each other and therefore are able to make eye contact, observe each other, empathize and harmonize with each other, and amplify the effects of the sacred sounds being produced. This symbolism also represents the spiral, which is a circle starting at a point at the middle and continuing its path forming concentric circles that are ever-widening and expanding. The coiled serpent is an icon that is seen in many ancient cultures as representing the expansion of consciousness from a single primordial point into the wider realms of existence. The image of the coiled serpent is seen in many cultures. The Aborigines used this imagery extensively, as do the Chinese in the form of the "Dragon dances". It's also found in icons found throughout Middle East, and in the ley lines and stone circles in Britain and other European countries, as well as in the more sophisticated form of mazes. So too with the music, which may start with a low, uninteresting fundamental note from which harmonic notes slowly emerge and become more sophisticated. As these sacred sounds become more enriched, with the production of more harmonics, so too does consciousness and the expansion of consciousness in a symbolic way.

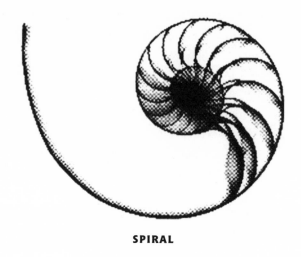

SPIRAL

The circle, and it's more complex form, the spiral, can be projected from a two dimensional structure into three dimensions so that instead of simply spiraling in a flat plain, if the spiral is seen to progress vertically upwards while expanding, it psychologically comes to represent not only expanded consciousness, but expansion into the heavens, or the ethereal and spiritual dimensions of existence. It is said that the rhythmic drumming, the clear whistles of harmonic Overtone singing, the ponderous drone of the didgeridoo, the pure tinkling notes of chimes and pure crystal "singing" bowl, act as a catalyst to focus and concentrate the body and mind into the task of approaching these trance-like states of expanded awareness and spirituality. In many ways, sacred sounds are considered to be the keys to open doors to the other dimensions of our lives that transcend our physical beings.

'2'

Different traditions in different parts of the world

To explore the ancient traditions
based on sound and harmonies, our journey
needs to take us to Asia and beyond.

CENTRAL ASIA

PEOPLE HAVE INHABITED the Altai region of eastern Turkey since time immemorial. There is evidence of human settlement that precedes even the first ice age. In the town Gorno-Altaisk there is a Paleolithic site estimated as being between 900,000 & 800,000 years old. This mountainous region is in western Siberia, bounded by Mongolia, China, Kazakistan and Russia. The Altai Mountains are still remote and relatively inaccessible even today. These golden (Altai literally means golden) mountains are especially known for their spectacular and unspoilt natural beauty. In the context of spectacular landscapes with soaring mountains, crashing and splashing rivers and waterfalls, and a huge diversity of animal and plant wildlife, it is easy to see how inspirational ideas, coupled closely to natural phenomena, evolved. It was surrounded by this natural beauty that legends and myths evolved among the predominantly nomadic people who have lived there since the beginning of time.

This region has been the crossroads and a melting pot in which different tribes and peoples came into contact with one another and intermingled. Tribal wars were a frequent occurrence, with Mongolian armies sweeping eastwards on horseback (known to us as the Huns), Semitic tribes from Persia and Mesopotamia moving north, Turkish (Altian) tribes spreading in every direction, and Germanic Aryan tribes moving east and south. As societies matured and the warring tribes settled down, trade developed between the regions giving an exchange of ideas, religions, art and musical traditions. The most extensive trading network in this region was known as the "Silk Route" which extended from China in the East through to the Mediterranean in the West.

Much of our Western culture originated in Asia. It is here that traditionally the Garden of Eden was placed (there is still a region in north-western Iran/north-eastern Iraq known even today as the Garden of Eden). Noah's Ark came to rest on Mount Ararat,

Abraham set out from Ur, and the whole of the Old Testament story unfolded from there. It is in many parts of this region that ancient traditions are maintained even today. Many communities exist in the remote parts of Central Asia stretching across from Turkey to Mongolia, Siberia and Tibet, which have hardly been affected by the passage of time. The remote communities of Karakalpakstan, Uzbekistan, and Kazakhestan and the Bashkir communities all have very similar cultural origins. From the Ural Mountains in the east to the Himalayas and Altai Mountains bordering Tuva, these people have lived close to nature for centuries, caring for their pastoral animals, and growing subsistence crops. There are traditions related in epic stories and poems. There is also a long history of singing, often to the accompaniment of rudimentary instruments to supply either a drum beat, or some notes of music to give a consistent pitch and melody. Many of the singing traditions throughout this region are based on the use of fundamental humming or droning notes overlaid by harmonic Overtones achieved by either controlling the air passing through the nose, or the mouth, or both. Therefore styles differ greatly, as do the melodies and a harmonics produced.

Turkic-speaking Baskirs who live in communities in the Ural mountains call their style of singing *uzlyau*, while the Khakass, further to the west call their singing technique *khai*, and the Mongolians and Tuvinians even further to the west, call their style *khoomei*.

The *khai* technique is a well-developed and ancient technique that is at the heart of many communal functions. It is bound up in tradition and heritage and is usually performed by a single male singer. Often performed on horseback, and occasionally using some accompaniment, the technique produces a very low droning fundamental note together with a high-pitched, whistling, Overtone note. Performances last for several hours, or even several days. Performers use this medium not only to produce entertaining and melodious performances, but more importantly to relate historic and traditional stories. This singing technique is also used ritualistically for prayer, thanksgiving and invocation of the spirits of nature. Historic stories, poems, songs and ancient wisdom are conveyed to the listeners during such performances.

AUSTRALIAN ABORIGINES

THE AUSTRALIAN ABORIGINAL culture has developed the use of sacred sounds to connect with ethereal images to a very high level. The Aborigines are made up of a number of different tribes with different traditions. Some anthropologists believe that their origins may be related to the Eastern metaphysical traditions because of great similarities that exist between their mystical traditions and those of India. The most studied, and it would seem the most sophisticated, tribes are those in the north and north west of Australia, particularly in the Kimberley region. These tribes induce trance-like states by using the didgeridoo.

This instrument is essentially a hollowed out piece of wood that, when blown properly, creates a deep echoing drone from which a rich range of harmonic Overtones are produced. In producing these sacred tones, participants enter "dreamtime".

Mystical mouthless individuals called Wandjina inhabit this timeless and formless dimension. These individuals are represented in the numerous rock and cave paintings in this area. They vary enormously in their rendition from animal-like forms or composite animal and human forms, together with other images such as serpents. Many of these images, and the beings themselves in "dreamtime" are thought to represent the vital forces of nature and the Universe. The maintenance of these images, by their annual renewal, and the regular practice of engaging with these ethereal beings are crucial to the Aboriginal concept of maintaining personal well-being, well-being of the family, clan and tribe. Not only that, but also the general well-being of the country, with ample rainfall, regeneration of the earth in springtime, provision of abundant food, fertility and harmony in nature are promoted and energized. Experienced didgeridoo players are able to manipulate the sounds that they produce to emulate animal sounds and other sounds of nature to focus the group on particular aspects of nature being invoked. Similarly, imagery of rainbows (a phenomenon of awe among most peoples), and fire and snakes (which come out of dark holes in the Earth - likened to the womb – and are associated with creative energy, regrowth and fertility), feature highly in concentrating the mind to this task.

The physical phenomena of nature, and all of the physical objects in nature, especially the rocks and caves with their paintings and images are infused with the essential spirits of nature. By contemplating these images, an expansion of consciousness during rituals based on sacred sounds and movements, is amplified in the minds of participants. Even more importantly, it is believed that the communal release of this concentrated spiritual energy in the group harmonizes with the natural oscillations of the rocks and their images, stimulating their physical energy potential which in turn echoes into the spiritual realms that they represent. By engaging with the harmonious vibrations of nature itself, the Aborigines believe that they are able to change their environment and themselves to their mutual benefit. The sacred sounds produced by the didgeridoo harmonized into the group participating in the ritual with its imageries of nature are further enhanced by decorating the bodies of the performers and participants to represent those specific aspects of nature being invoked creating a total experience of visual, physical, mental, psychological, and sonic harmony.

NATIVE AMERICAN INDIANS

IN MUCH THE same way as the nomadic tribes and peoples of Tuva and Mongolia, the Altai Mountain regions of Turkey, the Aborigines in Australia, and the African tribes, the indigenous populations of the American Continent lived close to nature and their lives were intertwined with it. These indigenous people go under different names in different parts of America. In the far north they are called Inuit (Eskimos), and in Canada they are called the First Nations, whereas in the USA they are called Native Americans. In South America they are divided into two main groups, the Lowland (i.e. Amazon Basin), and Highland (i.e. Andean) that include many other groups from ancient times such as the Mayans, the Aztecs, and the Incas. Irrespective of the nomenclature, these indigenous peoples are made up of dozens of tribes, within which there were many sub-groups, each with its own traditions and rituals, religions, and gods. It is therefore impossible in a short work such as this to describe in detail the different musical traditions of the plethora of tribes that make up this vast and diverse group of people. At best, only the broadest of overview of the musical traditions of these peoples can be given.

These nomads were blessed with a good climate, and plentiful food. They were acutely aware of their good fortune, and as their lives were so closely intertwined with nature they felt that they were an integral part of this reality. They felt that their souls and spirits were part and parcel of the souls and spirits of the animals and vegetation, the mountains and the rivers, and indeed the very ground that they walked on. They were aware of and sensitive to, the uniqueness of different animals and plants, and in religious practice they invoked the spirits and souls of these living entities to the benefit of the tribe, or to pay homage and to give thanks to the spirits of nature that had endowed them with such good fortune. In general, birds (particularly the mythical Thunderbird) were associated with the heavens, the sun and rain, whereas other animals such as the coyote were closely associated with the earthly matters and yet other animals such us snakes were associated with the underworld. Most of the musical traditions occur around a circle of people around a campfire with singing or chanting and sometimes dancing and singing.

Most of indigenous American music is vocal. with relatively little reliance on musical instruments. A notable exception is drumming which almost always accompanies singing, although in many groups rattles are used as well. Some nations, but not all, use simple musical bows, flutes, whistles, or chimes to provide melodious accompaniment to the singing. Striking sticks, rasps and rattles are also sometimes used to maintain and amplify the rhythms of the song. Among the Southern American nations more complex flutes, panpipes and simple trumpet-like instruments are common. Some nations have developed styles based on solo performances by a leader, whereas others have developed musical traditions based on a call-and-response technique of a soloist and chorus, alternating responses.

The most common singing form is communal, sitting around a central campfire. As the concept of harmonies and harmonious Overtones is rare in most of these groups, everybody sings at the same pitch and tone. The traditions of harmonic Overtone singing and chanting, developed to such a high-level as in the East are virtually unknown throughout the American continent. Singing is therefore usually based on melodies alone, with variations in rhythm and pitch. As in other ancient cultures singing is the primary means of invoking the forces of nature. In most tribes singing is seldom used for recreational purposes, but is almost always used for a specific religious or social purpose.

Particularly in the South American nations, epic songs describing the history of the group and its mythological traditions are sung in addition to those used to bring good fortune to the tribe, those used for important life-cycle and social events, and those used for religious ceremonial and invocation purposes. In some nations the songs were used in a sarcastic tone as a defence against outsiders, whether neighboring tribes or, more importantly, directed at colonial Europeans who had encroached on their physical and spiritual lives.

In some nations songs are sung with real and meaningful words. However, in many traditions, meaningless sounds (called vocables) are chanted. While traditions vary, it is generally held that songs and music were, and still continue to be, introduced through dreams and visions from the spirit world to create sacred sounds that can be used by humans when they needed help. These sacred sounds vary between different peoples and tribes in accordance with the spirits that surround them and protect them and so they are specific for each tribe or group. In these traditions it is crucial to create the right sounds, rather than convey a verbal story or meaning as in the case of traditions elsewhere. The sounds in current use have evolved over many years and are thought to have a deep mystical significance and sacred symbolism to invoke the spirits of nature. Similarly, the rhythms do not maintain a constant frequency, but are irregular and varied. The melodies therefore sound inconsistent in both rhythm and purity of tones. Buzzing, irregular tones in short sequences, often using no more than two different tones, are endlessly repeated by the group. This communal singing is often accompanied by dancing. When singing is accompanied by dancing, repetitive rhythms that are easy followed by participants are a characteristic. These simple melodies and simple rhythms make it easy for members of the group to participate, and can create hypnotic, trance-like states within the group. Using simple short repetitive sequences of steps, with many people crowded together and moving and singing in harmony the dancers may dance for hours on end until physical and/or emotional exhaustion enables them to transcend their normal conscious state. In this state, the spirits of nature may be placated, or invocations for help solicited, to overcome the difficulties of individuals or the community. Because of the sacred and mystical nature of the singing and dancing, the rhythms, dance routines, actions of the leaders and performers are usually beyond the comprehension of those who do not have an intricate knowledge of the traditions and beliefs of the specific community being observed. There is a degree of spontaneity within these musical traditions, so that often the songs and the dancers may follow unpredictable sequences, but these are in fact not unlike the syncopated changes that occur continuously in jazz music. In jazz, a standardized musical sequence is embellished and reworked giving new and different interpretations of the same piece of music. This is symbolically the same as what happens in some of the singing and dancing routines, insofar as the subtle changes or the growth of embellishments and spontaneous, unexpected variations lead to greater insights and possibly messages from the spirit world. Most of all these communal ritualistic practices serve to strengthen and harmonize the bonds between participants had their Creator and Guardian spirits, themselves, their communities, and other communities.

Different performers often consider their songs to be their own personal property as they are specific to them and their relationship to the spirit world, while other songs and music belong to the clan or the tribe on a communal basis. Musical pieces are sometimes transmitted or exchanged with other neighboring groups. Therefore the traditions of one group may become dispersed in the integrated into the traditions of another. Songs and dances and music that have particularly powerful properties of healing, communication with the spiritual world, or invoking the forces of nature have slowly filtered through many regions to extend across different tribal boundaries through vast areas of the Continent. It is true that some of the music, songs, dances, and even concepts are adapted to the culture and religious practice of the adoptive group, but the essence remains unchanged. Musical traditions are passed on from father to son, or may be purchased, bartered or given away by performers to ensure the continuity of the musical traditions for posterity.

Regional variations of Overtone singing

From a musical point of view, the North American "Indian" nations can be divided into six broad regions in addition to the Highland and Lowland groups of southern Americans. The six regions in the USA are divided into: Eastern Woodlands, Plains, South-West, Great Basin, North-East Coast, and Arctic (according to the *Encyclopedia of North American Indians*)

Some of the **Highland South American** nations have developed techniques that are a more sophisticated forms of singing often accompanied with more sophisticated instruments such as panpipes.

In some groups, particularly in the **southern states** of the USA, very sophisticated singing and dancing rituals have been developed to create cohesive harmony among the participants, and harmony with their natural surroundings. Singing and dancing have been developed into sophisticated epics and plays that may last for hours, or in some cases days on end. In some of these nations, songs are used for recounting anything from trade and hunting, to encouraging goodwill and harmony between people and groups of people. These tribes also make extensive use of flutes, and may also include other artistic representations such as sand painting, to help visualize the spiritual images being invoked during their rituals. Other traditions include game-like dance rituals to enhance feelings of communality, and physical and spiritual harmony within the group.

In those nations in the **northeastern** parts of the USA, humorous and entertaining songs and dances with sophisticated instrumental accompaniment are used for social and entertainment purposes in addition to ritualistic uses.

The nations in Florida and in the **southeast** of the USA, use specific ritualistic dancing and singing the techniques. Characteristically the dances are highly rhythmic with repetitive stamping of feet and known as "stomp" dancing. Dancing is often accompanied by songs of communal harmony, personal healing and well-being and they are unique in that they rely on call-and-response techniques in which the soloist calls the tune and a chorus responds with the same repetitive chorus. With time the melodies have become more complex and varied, and can even include the use of harmonic Overtones to embellish simple melodies. As the music and dancing becomes more complex, so too does the state of well-being, heightened awareness, and hypnotic altered perception among the group. Further north, the music tends to be more relaxed, incorporating several scales and harmonies to achieve more melodious and harmonious musical styles.

Similarly those tribes in the **southwestern areas** also have sophisticated and highly stylized singing and dancing techniques. These songs and dances, accompanied by rhythmic drumming, tend to be slow and methodical, with humming fuzzy tones produced nasally.

The Plains area of the Great Prairie open spaces has a high-pitched formal and nasal style, forming a high-pitched buzz initially and then descending to lower pitches. Short musical phrases are repeated according to a pre-set choreography and accompanied by drums and sometimes flutes.

Great Basin and North-West Coast singers have a more relaxed and open vocal style. Harmonies are absent, with the sounds relying heavily on a melody usually being sung by a leader and a chorus repeating musical phrases in an alternating pattern. The songs are simple at first sight, but subtle, as the variations in tempo and melody created in the music are not immediately obvious. The variations in breathing techniques as occur in speech are sometimes reproduced in the melodies, producing rich and varied songs. Singing is usually accompanied by a variety of instruments to amplify and sustain the melody.

The Northern Arctic area has a style unlike that of any other regions and consists mainly of short repetitive musical phrases repeated to the rhythmic beating of tambourines and drums.

'3'

Introduction to
Tuvinian Overtone singing

SINCE THE EARLY 1970s and 80s, an interest in esoteric religions has grown among many people who have become increasingly disenchanted with the meaningless and shallow rituals of Western religious practice, the materialistic egocentricity of Western society, and who have a general feeling of alienation towards society, the excesses of authority (whether secular or religious), and communality in general.

Out of these feelings of aggressive alienation together with an absence of any true religious or spiritual fervor, movements such as the New Age movement were born and grew. These movements were (and still are) looking for something else! Something beyond the shallow materialism of Western society! Something more caring and/or inclusive of people as individuals and communities. This search has focused on Eastern religions, with their emphasis of meditative techniques, retuning, or re-harmonizing the spirit to the universal soul, and ultimately physical, psychological, and spiritual healing and well-being. The fascination with the sounds of Mongolian and Tibetan harmonic techniques has led to such terms as a "sonic meditation" and "re-harmonizing personal energy fields". The strange sounds, the hypnotic drone of the fundamental note, interjected with harmonic whistles and sounds of the accompanying instruments have been widely advertised as meditative ways of achieving magical, spiritual, and physical healing.

Overtone singing, harmonic-Overtone singing and throat singing are all names for a technique of singing in which different notes are sounded simultaneously by one person. The idea of a throat-singing group, with instruments, is new in Tuva and it has become popular by artists trying to copy or Westernize this technique. Sometimes instrumental accompaniment enhances the effect, but usually it is used to overcome the limitations of voices that have not achieved the rigorous demands on the vocal chords of the performers. When used for healing and meditation purposes, instrumental accompaniment is not used.

Khoomei is the name used in Tuva and Mongolia to describe a large family of singing styles and techniques known as throat singing. It is pronounced nearly identically in both regions, although Tuva and Mongolia use different languages, the technique is called *koomeiawsill* and is usually transliterated as *khoomay, khoomii, xoomii, koomii, xomej, höömeï*. Western terms for *khoomei* include harmonic singing, Overtone singing, diaphonic singing, or bi-phonic singing, all of which refer to similar but not necessarily identical vocal techniques.

Overtone singing is a form of chanting based on sounding one note and then magnifying the harmonic notes based on that note by changing the shape and flow of breath through the resonant cavities of the mouth, larynx, throat and nose.

Throat singing is found in many regions including Tuva (*khoomei*), Mongolia (*xoomej*) Kakhassia (*xai*), Bashkortstan, South Africa, Tibet (Tantric chants), Australia and others in which ritual singing is practiced.

ORIGINS AND BACKGROUND

IN THE REPUBLIC of Tuva and Mongolia the nomadic herders have been chanting *khoomei* for over a thousand years. The monks of the monastery of Gyütö in Tibet have a similar chanting practice known as the "yang" style and the monks in Drepung Loseling call it "zu-kay". The Xhosa women in South Africa call their style of chanting *umngqokolo*.

In Tuva, the "karguiraa" style of *khommei* singing is supposed to have been inspired by the imitation of a female Bactrian camel calling out for a lost calf. The Gyütö monks have been chanting in the "yang" style since around AD 1470 when Je Tsong Khapa founded the monastery. He was the originator of the style, said to have been inspired by the Chadruma (female deities). It is not yet known when or why the Xhosa women started to sing *umngqokolo*.

It is thought that many of these chanting styles arose from the nomadic herders who imitated the sounds around them as they watched their flocks of sheep, yaks, reindeer and camels. They listened to the sounds of the wind, the mountains, the creeks, the rustling grass, and imagined the many spirits surrounding them. The Tibetan monks, used this as part of the preparation for prayer as a way to cleanse themselves to pray to their deities.

A DESCRIPTION OF OVERTONE/THROAT SINGING

ESSENTIALLY, OVERTONE OR throat singing is a form of singing in which Overtones (i.e. harmonics) are created simultaneously by a single voice. This is generally known as *khoomei* though it is really only one of three or four styles. The basic note (called the fundamental) is a deep humming groan, mixed with a high-pitched whistling sound of the harmonic Overtones. Usually two or three "voices" are heard emanating from a single singer who may then sound like a group of three or even four separate singers. Tuvinians speak of "respect for ancestors" and "closeness to nature" and "sincerity" when speaking about their music.

In Mongolia and Tuva, the word *khoomei* means pharynx, or throat, and *khoomeilakh* is the technique of producing vocal harmonics. This is a physically demanding technique, that takes the human voice to its limits, but also requires the muscular control to control the flow of air through the throat, mouth, nose.

GEOGRAPHY

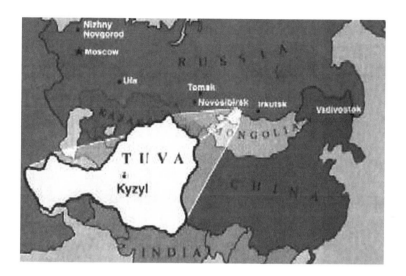

THE MOST WELL known throat singers are in the Republic of Tuva (now officially called Tyva), which is within Russia, bordering on Mongolia. This region is in the southern part of Siberia, in central Asia. It is bounded by the Altai Mountains and the Yenisei River in the north west and it is surrounded by mountain ranges on the north east, north, north west, and western boundaries. Tuva was therefore an isolated region, largely unaffected by outside influences. The capital city is Kyzyl, which is 800 meters above sea level. The rest of the country is flat grassland about 1,000 meters above sea level, except in the Sayan mountain regions to the South. The population of Tuva is approximately 310,000. The Tuvinans are largely nomadic herders, dependent on their flocks of sheep, reindeer, horses, and yaks, for food, clothing, warmth and protection from the weather. Their culture is closely related to that of Mongolia's, but the Tuvinians take pride in proclaiming their differences from their neighboring Mongolians. Tuvinians have distinctly Far-Eastern, Japanese-type features.

Other local regions in which throat singing is practiced include the **Altai region**, and most parts of western Mongolia. Other areas in Asia include, Turkic-speaking tribes from the Ural Mountains, known as the **Bashkirs**, and singers in Uzbekistan, Karakalpakstan and Kazakhstan who include harmonic Overtone singing techniques in their epic songs. Beyond Asia, the use of harmonic, Overtone singing techniques is not common, but it is practiced in other parts of the world.

Rooted in its shamanistic past, the origins of *khoomei* are explained in several ways. It is claimed the isolated areas of Mongolia with their unusual features of nature seen in the mountains, lakes, rivers and birds together with the intrinsic link to the magical or supernatural, gave rise to this style of singing. The region known as Chandman Sum is particularly isolated. It is surrounded on three sides by mountains and lakes, and by a river called Chono Xaraix. To the south lies semi-desert of Mongolia.

IGIL BEING PLAYED

A number of accompanying instruments have gradually been introduced, of which the most common is the *byzaantzy* (a crude violin like instrument played with the hairs of the bow threaded between the strings, and common local instruments including the "horsehead" fiddle, *igil* (pronounced ih-gill) which commemorates a mountain pony of legendary fame and is one of the most ancient and popular musical instruments.

It is made from the mane hair of this animal. Conch shells, shaman rattles and drums may be used as accompaniment. Other instruments include the *ediski*, a single reed that makes sounds like a female musk deer; *khirlee*, a thin piece of wood that is spun like a propeller to sound like the wind; *amyrga*, a hunting horn that sounds like the mating call of a stag; and *chadagan*, a zither that hums in the wind when Tuvinian herders place it on the roofs of their tents.

Players of the *khomus*, or "Jew's harp" (or more correctly a Jaw Harp), create natural sounds, like rushing water, but also human speech like sounds. Siberian groups make use of many more instruments, especially drums.

Throat singing is used by nomads of the region to focus on, and tune into, their natural acoustic environment. They have cultivated this tradition as a form of communication between themselves, the spirits and natural phenomena around them, which they try to imitate with their voices.

A SHORT HISTORY OF THROAT SINGING

Mongolia and Siberia

The most powerful religious belief in these countries has always been shamanism, a religion based on a closeness and unity with nature. Tibetan Buddhism supplanted this, and during the Communist regimes of the 1930s, all religion was eliminated. However, shamanism continued to be practiced in secret.

Shamanism has always been a national religion in Tuva. Men *and* women can become shamans. The shamanistic ritual (known as *kham*), has a monotonous chant, accompanied by a

large drum (called a *dungur*) with rattles attached. The art of playing the drum is special. The central technique of shamanism, found also in the Tibetan "Bon" rituals, is the imagery of a religious "flight" to the world beyond, which is induced by means of drumming, chanting and singing. Historically the techniques probably evolved from the use of magic chants to call spirits to the shaman, the idea of flight into the spirit world being a later development.

Although the true genesis of throat singing as practiced today is obscure, Tuvinian pastoral music is intimately connected to an ancient tradition of animism. This is the belief that natural objects and phenomena have souls or are inhabited by spirits. According to Tuvinian animism, the spirituality of animals, mountains and rivers are manifested not only through their physical shape and location but also through the sounds they produce. The wind howling around the mountains is given spiritual significance. Animals, too, are said to express spiritual power sonically. Humans can tune in to this power, amplify it, and even manipulate it, by imitating these sounds of nature. Proximity to nature produces a dependency on Tuva's resources and an intimate relationship of respect for the spirituality of the natural world. This sense of intimacy is very much reflected in *khoomei*, the Tuvinian form of throat or Overtone singing.

Mongolian folklore has a beautiful story regarding the origins of *khoomei*: A very important bird in this region is the Usny Buxl bittern. According to one story, this bird buries its head beneath the surface of the lake and then sings. *Khoomei* is sometimes referred to as "bird's echo." The Mongolians also stress that the sounds heard in the mountains have a special quality. For instance, Mount Jargalant is said to be able to "hold" the very strong winds that come from the west before releasing them into the steppe below. Sometimes the wind is held for four to five hours whilst at other times the duration is said to last for three days. This gives warning to the people living in that area. During this time the mountain drones or makes a hollow sound. Older people from the area credit the same power to the lakes saying that Mount Jargalant and Lake Xar Us Nuur "attract and digest the sound of the wind". Some even speak of a musical communication existing between these two. In this region there are many waterfalls and rivers that produce different combinations of sounds depending upon the type of stones over which they run. A particular river, the River Erv, is credited with magical properties and also as being the origin of this style of singing.

Siberian equestrian herdsmen had little variation in their daily activities and so they amused themselves and their families by singing, and also by reproducing the sounds of nature that they heard around them. They could not carry large instruments on horseback so *khoomei* developed as a vocal technique that was later embellished into the sophisticated forms that we hear today.

Other nomadic tribes of southern Siberia have practised throat singing for many centuries. Various forms of throat singing have been practiced by a number of Central Asian nomadic tribes such as the Huns, the Chacass, the Tuvinians, the Altaians, and the Mongols. These nomads were known in the West as the Scythians, a terrifying warlike group of tribes who, under the leadership of Attila the Hun, terrorised Europe for many years. In the Middle

Ages Genghis Khan lead Mongol armies against local Asian and Chinese countries. Finally, they reached Europe, where these oriental armies known as "The Tartars", waged brutal and bloody wars, and were greatly feared.

Traditionally both male and female singers practiced the art, but with time, throat singing was considered unsuitable for women because it was thought that due to the considerable muscle control centered on the abdomen and chest, pregnant women might miscarry while throat singing. This became an exclusively male occupation, although today women also perform *khoomei*.

Most of the Central Asian nomadic tribes were incorporated into the Soviet Union and these traditions and skills were discouraged, and were to a great extent, lost. After Soviet rule ended, several tribes regained their sense of national pride, and many of them, of which the best known are the Tuvinians, rediscovered their old traditions, including the traditional throat singing passed down by their ancestors. There has therefore been a resurgence of throat singing in neighboring regions in Western Mongolia. Variations of this technique are also practiced in Tibet

In addition to Tuvinian and Mongolian styles, Khakassian (xaj) and Gorno-Altaian *(kaj)"* Overtone singing, usually accompanying epic songs, should be mentioned. While Tuvinian, and to a lesser extent Mongolian, musicians travel around the world performing their *khoomei* style, very little is heard of other Central Asian styles such as the *"uzliau"* or *"tamak kurai"* styles of Bashkirs, who live in the European part of Russia, some few thousand kilometers from Tuva. Their style of Overtone singing includes melodies of ordinary folksongs. The Baskirs are a Turkic people, who moved from Central Asia in the first millennium and they brought with them this peculiar singing style when moving westward from Central Asia.

Tibet

According to legend, in AD 1433, the Tibetan lama, Je Tzong Sherab Senge, awoke from a dream in which he had heard a voice, droning unlike any sound that he had heard before. It was a low deep growl like drone. But there was a second accompanying voice that was high pitched and clear, like the notes of a flute. These two voices, seemed to come simultaneously from deep within himself.

In his dream, Je Tzong Sherab Senge had used this special sound as a new chanting style to focus divine energy. This "Tantric" voice was to be used as a prelude to prayer to unite those chanting with the divine consciousness.

The next morning, Je Tzong Sherab Senge began to chant, recreating the strange Tantric drone that he had heard in his dream. So it was that more that 500 years ago, the Gyume Tantric Monastery began in Lhasa, Tibet. The chanting monks of this monastery learnt how to chant three harmonic notes (i.e. Overtones) simultaneously, creating a "one voice chord". Shortly thereafter, another monastery in Lhasa, the Gyuto Tantric College, was founded. Similar chanting techniques were practiced at this monastery.

Throat singing in the West

In Mongolia, the general term for this singing is "khoomei" (khöömei, khoomii, (pronounced hoomi, choomi in the West, or hermai). Alternatively it is written as "chömei" ("ö" is pronounced like "o" and "e" simultaneously), which is translated as "throat." Because this technique requires the manipulation of the air flow through the throat to produce the harmonic Overtone, the term "throat singing", is not only a direct translation of the word khoomei, but it also describes the technique itself. The tradition of khoomei is acknowledged as being the most highly developed form of Overtone harmonic chanting. The chanting is reminiscent of the sound of a Jew's harp being played, producing a nasal droning, or humming sound. Simultaneously, another sound at a higher pitch (i.e. another note in the same harmonic scale) is sounded.

In English *khoomei* is therefore known as throat-singing. As there are many variations of this type of chanting, it is also known as Overtone singing, harmonic singing, split-tone singing or harmonic chanting.

STYLES OF TUVA OVERTONE SINGING

THE MONGOLS DID not have a traditional, general classification of their styles of Overtone singing. The late folklore specialists Badraa and the singer Tserendavaa attempted to make such a classification of Mongolian *khoomei*. Their results seem to be based on two criteria: the places of origin and the place of resonance in the body when singing *khoomei*. They described six different styles: *uruulyn* (labial) *khoomei, tagnain* (palatal) *khoomei, xamryn* (nasal) *khoomei, bagalzuuryn* (glottal or throat) *khoomei, tseejiin xondiin* or *xevliin* (chest cavity or stomach) khoomei and *turlegt or xosmoljin* khoomei (*khoomei* combined with a long and often epic song). The latter style is somewhat controversial, since different singers have different opinions about what constitutes it, and whether or not it is *khoomei* at all.

Tuva styles may be divided into various categories, of which the most common styles are basic *khoomei* (sounding like the wind swirling among rocks), *sygyt* (high tone; an imitation of the gentle breezes of summer; the songs of birds.), *kargyraa* (low tone; imitating the howling winds of winter; the plaintive cries of a mother camel after losing her calf), *borbangnadyr* (which means "rolling" and imitates either the sound of running water, or horses hooves) and *ezenggileer*. Tuva is a peculiar vocal art with three basic vocalizing methods and at least four sub-methods that allow a singer to simultaneously sing two, and often up to four voices notes simultaneously.

However, the Tuvinians acknowledge only three basic categories:

Khoomei. A vocal style that enables the singer to produce what sounds like several simultaneous voices: one fundamental with low sound produces a drone, with the simultaneous Overtones producing secondary melodies. *Khoomei* is the common term for Overtone singing, as it is the origin of all of the other styles. The English translation is "throat, pharynx". It is considered as the oldest style by many Tuvinian singers. Western singers have likened the sound of this technique as being like an American "howling wolf". This is because once the base note is sounded, the throat is tightened while pronouncing the alternating of vowel sounds "ooo-ahh-ooo-ahhh-ooo-ahhh", moving that tongue forward and backward to create the melodic Overtones. The lips are tightly pursed when intoning the vowel "ooo" and then relaxed when intoning the vowel "ahh". Traditionally this sound represented the sound of rushing streams of water swirling and over rocks and cataracts.

Sygyt (also written and pronounced Sigit, or Sygut). A high-pitched Overtone singing technique sounding like a flute, or a whistle. It is often accompanied by reading of a text. The term *sygyt* means "whistle". Songs in *Sygyt* style start without Overtones. In this technique, the throat is tightened while sounding the vowels "ooo-eee-ooo-eee". Traditionally this sound is supposed to represent an imitation of the songs of birds and the wind whistling across the grasslands. Usually, only two notes are produced, and the lips are held pursed forward as though saying the word "oh!"

Borbannadyr (pronounced bor-bung-nah-dur). *Borbanadyr* is sung from a low vibratory fundamental note in the bass or baritone range. It is characterized by a varying pulsating rhythm using the lips, tongue and throat to produce a number of harmonics in rapid succession. The English translation of the word from which it is derived, *borbanna*, is "to roll over". The singer creates a tremolo of Overtones. This singing style is supposed to represent the gentle cascading of water over cataracts and rocks.

Another two categories are described, but are less frequently found:

Ezenggileer. Songs in this style were usually sung when riding on horseback. The English translation of the word from which it derived *ezengi*, which means stirrup or bridle. To-day the *ezengileer* style is rarely performed as is very difficult. *Ezengileer* is produced by rapid vibrations of the lips, and is sung over a low fundamental. It creates soft shimmering Overtone melodies. Both the high (nasal) and low (throat) sounds are important. The alternation of the two different sounds seem to define the style. It is characterized by a pulsating galloping asymmetrical rhythm that imitates riding on horseback.

Kargyraa (also written *kargyrah*, and pronounced kar-guh-rah). This is a very low Overtone chant, using long, slow breathing while intoning open vowel sounds (e.g.: u, o, ö, a) The term *kargyraa* means "to expectorate", and it sounds almost like a low droning growl. This is the most complex and difficult style to master. In this style the lips vibrate slightly as though pronouncing the vowels "ohhh-ahhh" in a rapid alternating fashion while intoning a base note in the normal speaking range. This style produces harmonics that are lower than this note, sometimes called undertones, sounding like a deep and gruff voice. The sound emanates from deep down in the throat, almost from within the chest itself. The sound is supposed to imitate the howling winds of winter or the pathetic wailing of a camel that loses its calf. *Kargyraa* is an extremely low sound: to get an idea of *kargyraa*, imagine a voice that resembles the roaring of a lion, the howling of a wolf, and the croaking of a frog all at the same time. The Tuvinian word *kargyraa* is also given the meaning of "hoarse voice". It sounds a bit like clearing your throat, and it can be reproduced as a continuous clearing of the throat, almost cough like sound arising from the deepest part of the windpipe; consequently low tones will start resonating in the chest. Overtones are amplified by varying the shape of the mouth cavity and the position of the tongue.

Apart from the five main styles, there are several other sub-categories. These include *Opei-khoomei* (i.e. lullaby *khoomei* which sounds like the rhythm of rocking a baby to sleep), *khovu-kargyraa* (riding a horse with the wind blowing across the mouth), *dag-kargyraa* (a mountain echolike intonation), *chelbig-kargyraa* (sung while continuously moving a fan in front of the mouth to provide turbulence in the breath), *sygytting borbannadyr* (*sygyt* singing in *borbannadyr* style), *chilandyk* (a combination of *sygyt* and *kargyraa* alternating between high and low notes sounding a bit like a *chilandyk* (meaning cricket), *dumchuktaar* (meaning "from the nose" as this is how it is sung), *kangzyp* (a sad, wailing, irritating drone), and *xörekteer* (*xörek* means breast, because it is sung, usually with words, from deep within the chest).

Overtone singing in Tibet

Some Tibetan monasteries, especially those of Gyuto and Gyume, are famous for their mystical harmonic "tantras" (Buddhist intonations) that are chanted so that two or more harmonics are audible. The words of these tantras cannot be translated, because they have only symbolic meanings, giving them magical, and spiritually uplifting characteristics. This type of Overtone chanting uses a different chanting technique to the Mongolian styles. These Overtones are considered as ethereal and magical extensions of language, because they are uttered only when the tantras are sung. This style of chanting sounds a bit like Tuvinian *borbanndyr*.

Tibetan chanting uses mantric formulae derived from sacred texts. These mantras are an invocation to specific deities. The chanters visualize these deities while creating a circular cosmological painting which is called a Mandala. This enables the monks to become the embodiment of the energies they are invoking.

MANDALA

There are two styles of Overtone chanting in Tibet, developed by the monks of Gyütö and Gyüme tantric universities. The *dbyangs* (meaning based on vowels), style is a stunning form of voice production employed at the Gelugpa monastery, known to Westerners as "one-voice chording". The voice is unusually rich in harmonics. *Dbyangs* are "intoned" in drawn-out complex melodies and are the most highly valued, slowest paced, lowest pitched, most complex and most beautiful chants found in Tibetan Buddhist music. In Western terms, their melodies consist of sequences of smooth and continuously changing harmonic variations including changes of pitch, loudness, and harmonies. Some *dbyang* styles make prominent use of pitch variations, while others alter the resonating quality by sounding secondary syllables or text.

African spiritual and Overtone singing

Music, singing, and dancing, have strong traditions in Africa. Singing and dancing are used to serve many purposes, ranging from war dances to lullabies, and many others. Often the songs and tunes are used for ritualistic purposes. Chanting, ululations, and other vocal expressions often accompany births, deaths, initiation ceremonies and other life events. Chanting is often used by shamans and witch doctors to achieve heightened awareness or hypnotic states for prediction, elimination of the evil spirits, or connecting with the spirits of the past and present. Different tribes have different singing styles.

An area of particular interest is in the south-east of South Africa where the Zulu and Xhosa tribes live as neighbors.

Overtone singing in southern Africa:
Umngqokolo Ngomqangi.

In the case of the Zulu and Xhosa tribes of South Africa, singing and chanting have been developed to a high level, and used for recreational purposes as well as for religious events. These two tribes share much in common, but particularly they have a rich and highly developed musical tradition. The Zulu tradition is more closely rooted in music with a heavy beat that was often used for war dances to raise emotional fervor in warriors. Another very special technique that is highly developed is the "call-and-response" choral musical style, based on a small group of singers creating harmonies in response to a leader. Often these groups rely solely on their vocal acumen to achieve the necessary harmonies to produce a cohesive melody. However, it is not uncommon for accompaniment to be provided by hand clapping, rattles, simple single-string, violin-like instruments (called *uhadi, mhrube* in Xhosa, and *ugubhu* or *umakhweyana* in Zulu), or mouth harps (*isitolotolo*).

Mouth Harp

These violin-like instruments are nothing more than a gourd with an attached reed tensioning the single string, which is usually made of twisted grass. They are similar to many other instruments such as the *igil* used in Mongolia, and which are found in primitive cultures all over the world. When the string is plucked, its produces a humming sound which forms the fundamental on which the singers then superimpose the harmonic melody. A variation on this instrument is the jaw/mouth bow or harp (called an *isitolotolo*, or *umrubhe*). A more sophisticated variation is commonly found in the West is the "jaw" harp (Jew's") harp. With these instruments, instead of using a gourd as the resonating box to amplify and consolidate the fundamental note, the inside of the mouth is used instead. By changing the shape of the mouth, different notes can be produced and sometimes even some harmonics as well. It is also possible for the performer to whistle or hum simultaneously to produce different notes and melodious sounds. The notes produced are unclear, and sound more like a hum or drone rather than the crisp, clear notes produced by more sophisticated instruments such as a flute. By providing this underlying drone together with a drum like beat, performers can sing a melody on an harmonic scale based on the fundamental note and the rhythm created. Such techniques produce the characteristic sounds of Africa, in which groups of musicians and singers achieve their music, singing and dancing.

The Shona people, who live predominantly in Zimbabwi, had a religion based on a supreme being who could be contacted through the spirit world. In order to communicate with the spirit world the spiritual leader, a shaman, leader or witch doctor had to be possessed by an intermediary who could advocate the needs of the tribe to the ancestral spirits and the ultimate supreme being. Ceremonies to achieve this possession by the spirit were based on singing, dancing and hand clapping. In addition, drums were played incessantly at a very fast rhythm and melodies created with thumb pianos (called a *mbira*), simple xylophones (called a marimba) and other instruments based on gourds. As the *mbira* has only five notes, the music is simple in its structure, but its hypnotic effects are achieved by complex interlocking rhythms and beat patterns. Using a combination of rhythmic dancing, clapping and music, the group would be whipped up into frenzy, which was then concentrated on the leader who would then be able to receive the spirit being invoked. The musical sounds of the *mbira* had unique mystical sounds that were believed to have special resonances with the spirit world, creating an immediate direct "hotline" to the spirits. The *mbira* was used to invoke the spirits of ancestors, past tribal chiefs, guardians, rainmakers, and even to lift evil curses that were placed on the tribe, or to cure illnesses.

The Xhosa people however, have an especially rich and unique technique of Overtone singing. This has been extensively investigated by Dave Dargie (*Xhosa Music,* published 1988). The form of Overtone singing is reminiscent of the *kargyraa* style, and it is called *unngqokolo* in Xhosa. Generally the resonances and harmonics produced are unclear. One woman (Mrs Nowyilethi Mbizweni) has developed a particular style reminiscent of the humming or buzzing sound of the *umrubhe* mouth bow, with clear Overtone harmonics being produced. A childhood game, quite common among rural African children, is to impale a large beetle called in Xhosa the *umqangi* beetle on a small stick, and while the beetle, flapping its wings furiously to try to escape, produces a humming sound, it is placed in front of the mouth, that then focuses and amplifies the sound. Changing the shape of the mouth and lips can change this to produce a varying tonal hum. It is said that it was this sound that inspired Mrs Mbizweni to develop her sophisticated and unique technique of Overtone singing.

The Xhosa tribe is unique in the African continent, in their use of a highly evolved and unique culture of Overtone music used for ritualistic purposes. Unlike the Far-Eastern traditions, Overtone singing of the Xhosa is done by women. There is not a consistent pattern of singing throughout the tribe. It seems to be concentrated in several small villages. Xhosa women always sing in groups and tell simple stories of communal interest, usually with some admonition to wrongdoers. The technique, known as *unmgqokolo* (the *"go"* being sounded as a click sound in the Xhosa language), is often used for divination purposes and at major rituals such as during rites of passage for boys and girls. Another variation called *amaquisa* is used to contact departed ancestors.

The actual singing technique is different to that of the Mongolian and Tibetan chanting, although the sound of it is likened to the Mongolian *kargiraa* style. Instead of dividing the mouth and throat into different sectors that are manipulated separately to produce the rich range of harmonic Overtones in the Mongolian techniques, the Xhosa women use a simpler open/closed mouth technique, manipulating the volume of the sounds produced, with the mouth acting as a variable resonator. The primary musical instrument used by the Xhosa is the single stringed bow called an *uhadi*, and the technique of singing with Overtones was apparently derived from imitating the sound produced by this instrument. The instrument is similar to a single-stringed violin, and it emits a drone-like hum. The rich humming note consists of a fundamental, and some harmonic Overtones.

When singing, the fundamental note is sounded, and by altering the volume and mouth shape, an harmonic Overtone can be produced. Sometimes a second harmonic may sound as well. The technique does not produce the rich Overtone singing sounds of the Mongolians and Tibetans, but gives a rich polyphonic texture to the music.

THE SCIENCE OF TUVINIAN OVERTONE SINGING

X-RAY ANALYSIS, SONOGRAMS, and other spectral analysis techniques have been used to try and identify the mechanical processes that result in the production of harmonic Overtones when using such techniques as *khoomii*. Work, predominantly by Tran Quang Hai (National Centre for Scientific Research, Paris, France) has highlighted the differences in the different bony resonating cavities of the head, muscle contractions, and other soft tissue changes that occur during Overtone singing and simple vowel pronunciation. This research has shown that in Overtone singing, muscles of the stomach, chest, pharynx and nose all participate in producing the correct airflow, as well as manipulations of the tongue to alter the shape of the mouth and throat, and the subdivision between the upper and lower or front and back parts. The primary resonance arises in the vocal cords and this is then transmitted to either or both the pharynx and the mouth, where the secondary harmonic Overtones are produced.

There is a body of research comparing this similarity of the fundamental resonating note to the tone produced by the mouth or "jaw"(Jew's) harp. In both cases, it is the shape of the mouth and the position of the tongue that changes the characteristics of the resonance and produces the harmonic Overtones above the fundamental drone. Using a "jaw" or mouth harp is a less demanding and simpler way of producing the initial resonating fundamental note than techniques such as *khoomei* which takes considerable practice to achieve and demands extreme muscle control. Because of the extreme demands made on the singer, there is some evidence that damage may occur to the delicate vocal cords and mucosa (the skin lining the inside of the pharynx and windpipe) particularly by those unpracticed in the art, or who attempt to force the sustained production of Overtones.

Vocal chords, lips, tongue, diaphragm, chest, abdominal muscles and other parts of the body are all used in throat singing. In Mongolia the best singers are also often the best wrestlers!

It requires considerable strength to perform the technique well. The concept that a single performer can simultaneously sing two or more notes is beyond the perception of most people in the West. Usually, several performers are required to perform a multi-vocal concert. No two people can ever have the same timbres due to anatomical variations in the throats and mouths of individuals. The rich individual character of people's voices arise as a result of harmonic Overtones that resonate in the windpipe and air chambers of the respiratory tract during sound production from the vocal chords.

Overtone singing techniques require a single vocalist to produce at least two distinct tones simultaneously. One tone is a low, sustained drone of the fundamental note, with the series of whistle-like harmonics, which resonate at notes above the fundamental buzz may be musically altered to sound like chirp of a bird, the rushing water of a mountain stream or the sounds of a cantering horse. The sound produced has been likened to the drone of a bagpipe with a tune superimposed on the base note, or a jaw harp, in which a base note is sounded, and subsidiary notes are obtained by altering the shape and tension of the mouth.

There is also some evidence that simply listening to the Tuvinian sounds and concentrating on their resonances may have a beneficial effect without the necessity to actually have mastered the technique itself. But whether this is true, or even to what extent it may be true has not been determined.

In Mongolia the ancient shamanistic practices are still used today. The whistling sound of the harmonic Overtones that arise from the Overtone singing techniques in Tuva are especially revered for calling up or communicating with the spirits of the mountains, lakes, and other natural phenomena, in what is still largely a nomadic community, highly dependent on nature for its very survival.

'4'

Western adaptations

OVERTONE SINGING IS considered by some to be harmonic singing with the intentional emphasis on the non-fundamental harmonic notes. There is a category commonly known as "Western Overtone singing" that utilizes vowels, mouth shaping, and upper throat manipulations such as rotation of the hyoid bone to produce melodies and textures. In most cases, this produces a sound that is mildly guttural, with clear, but soft harmonics. There is often a strong nasal component, and a generally diffuse buzzing sound.

There are a number of Western classical schools that have tried to integrate the sounds of Overtone singing into Western music. One of the best-known classical composers is the German composer Karlheinz Stockhausen. He composed a work first performed in December 1968 entitled *Stimmung*, which was based on Overtone singing. The inspiration for this harmonic choral work was derived from the invocation of magical powers, and the gods of the people of Mexico. Other workers in this field such as David Hykes have related their music to "gravity waves", "solar winds", and even sunshine itself.

The first written records of *khoomei* are found in the sixteenth century. A few recordings of this vocal technique from Mongolia were released in the West during the early 1970s. Subsequently David Hykes from New York has specialized in developing this technique within a musical context. He created the "Harmonic Choir" in New York in 1975. They meet at the Church of St John the Divine and they have produced several albums. David Hykes and his Harmonic Choir use the Overtones to link with the cosmic Universe in his compositions. He has also experimented with numerous styles and techniques, including changing the fundamental base note introducing text, and musical instruments. Other groups of singers have also succeeded in creating simple Overtone singing techniques, and several vocal pieces in this category. Recordings of these techniques are freely available.

Using such techniques as pioneered by David Hykes, the possibility of using vowel sounds to generate harmonic resonances with spiritual realms has been extensively explored. We all intone vowels automatically in our daily speech: inability to do so would make communication impossible. However, intoning vowels and vowel sequences in such a way as to generate harmonic resonances and Overtones does not come naturally. It takes a great deal of practice and discipline in enunciating the sounds in such a way as to achieve a balance between the sound produced by the vocal cords, the tension in the facial muscles, and the shape and position of the lips and tongue. As each of us is slightly different, the basic note (i.e. the fundamental) is pitched slightly differently, and the overtoning harmonic resonances will similarly be slightly different. This is obvious if one considers how no two voices are exactly the same. As the fundamental note and its harmonics produced by each individual are slightly different and unique to that individual, the sonic fingerprint of each person is different, and therefore unique to that person. In the technique used by David Hykes, a humming sound based on a letter such as "m" is sounded to create the fundamental note at a natural and relaxed pitch. The pitch may be varied until a natural or comfortable resonance is felt in the body. While humming "mmmmm ..." the lips are slightly parted, introducing the possibility of creating a vowel sound overlying the fundamental note created by the humming sound. By changing the positions and altering the muscle tone of the cheeks and possibly of the jaw and tongue, an harmonic sound will sooner or later be produced. Once the first harmonic Overtone is produced, it is possible to create higher harmonic notes by subtly altering the shape and position of the lips and muscles around the position of the initial harmonic sound produced.

In Western music, there have been a number of musical pioneers who have explored the sonic contours of the human voice. Meredith Monk, Leon Thomas, Diamanda Galas, Joan La

Barbara, and Bobby McFerrin have made careers out of finding out what vocal chords can reverberate into besides words. In a different way, the gospel exhortations of soul singers have explored the human range of emotion, using different choral and harmonic techniques.

The cowboys of the Wild West had a great tradition of singing and dancing. Cowboys also live and work close to nature like the nomads of Tuva, Mongolia etc. However, their singing has not naturally developed into sounds mimicking nature. Often yodeling was substituted for words or used as an accompaniment in songs and melodies. This produced the characteristically catchy sounds of many of these songs. In the 1920s, an accomplished singer called Arthur Miles experimented with the use of Overtone singing in cowboy songs, dispensing with the yodeling sounds that were so popular. This produced the strange amalgam of voice, guitar and a strangely abrasive and undulating drone that sounds unique and particularly strange to the Western ear.

According to some Western enthusiasts such as David Hykes, Overtone singing works best in an environment where the Overtones can be amplified in the surrounding space. According to these practitioners, heightened spirituality is generated in the physical resonances in the body or "lives" in the "spaces" between notes.

'5'

How to "do it yourself"

THE SCIENCE OF TUVINIAN OVERTONE SINGING

KHOOMEI SINGERS INITIALLY create a low resonating vibrato base note in their lower throats (i.e. in effect using their false vocal chords - in effect in their chests), then, at the same time an harmonic Overtone is created using their true vocal cords and/or upper throats to produce a whistle-like tone at a higher pitch than the base note, but in harmony with it. By changing the shape of their throats, pharynx, mouths, and lips and redirecting the flow of air in different directions, these singers alter the harmonic sounds that they produce. The fundamental base note is maintained as a low-pitched drone in the vocal chords. Because the sounds emanate from the throat, and are then harmonized higher up in the mouth. This style is also known as throat singing.

The *khoomei* singer varies his throat and cheek muscles to create different harmonies (i.e. Overtones) caused by varying the airflow across the vocal chords, inside the mouth, around the tongue and through the slightly parted lips. As a result, variable pitched harmonics are produced to form a whistle-like melody, which is "sung" above the humming base note.

It is necessary to tighten the throat muscles to restrict the fundamental audible bass tone. This allows the Overtones to dominate the melody. Usually, only a very faint harmonic melody is produced above a relaxed and more dominant base tone which may drown out the melody altogether.

HOW YOU CAN DO IT

This is how you can learn to hum and sing *khoomei*:

Essentially, you sound a humming note with tightening of the "false" vocal chords (i.e. deep in the throat or even the chest, below the vocal cords themselves).

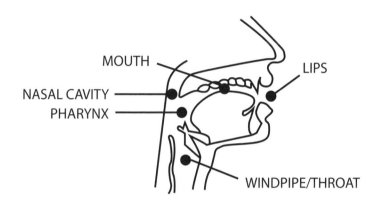

Throat diagram

The hum or drone must have a steady controlled strength. When you are relaxed and the sound is steadily droning, open your lips, mouth and throat slightly. You have now created a resonating chamber in the mouth and throat. Change the shape and position of your lips, throat, cheeks and tongue until flute-like whistling Overtones occur. You need to practice and experiment with different positions and sounds because in the beginning your Overtones will be weak or hardly exist. In fact few people can produce a strong enough Overtones to hear when they first start.

With regular daily practice, you will be able to produce the Overtones, but it may take as long as a few months before you will achieve a tuned *khoomei* voice.

Learning other styles

Sygyt has its roots in the *khoomei* -method. To practice *sygyt* you must start with *khoomei*. Singing *khoomei*, place the tip of your tongue behind your front teeth as if pronouncing the letter "L"; then press sides of your tongue against your upper teeth and half-open your mouth. Now you may be puzzled to realize that you no longer can utter a sound. However, if you keep your tongue in the described position you have a different resonating chamber in your mouth. If you now make a little opening to the seal between your tongue and your palate and sound a strong, constrained hum you may hear a clear flute-like Overtone. This miraculous Overtone is actually as clear as the sound heard when a wine glass is clinked! People who are not familiar with this sound, hardly believe that what they hear is a human voice. At your first attempt you will find that keeping your tongue in that position and trying to produce any sound is almost impossible. However, with practice you will be able to produce these Overtones

Siberian singers in particular, have learnt to constrict the lower part of their throats, known as the false vocal chords, and to vary the shape of their mouths and tongues to produce a number of different harmonic notes. Some of these Overtones are deep buzzing and humming sounds, while others are distinct and clear, like the sound of a flute. Whenever a person makes a sound, the blending of the harmonic notes gives the characteristic quality of a person's voice. Similarly, if the vowels a, e, i, and o, are pronounced at the same pitch, we are able to distinguish them because of their characteristic harmonic (i.e. Overtone) profiles. By constricting the vocal chords, some of the Overtones in the person's voice can be magnified and emphasised while the droning bass note is suppressed.

To achieve throat singing, it is necessary to carefully practice controlled breathing and to be physically fit. Singing should not be done immediately after a large meal, the mouth should be free of moisture and food debris, and you should avoid very cold food before singing. It is important to create the right state of consciousness, and be spiritually sensitive, and at peace with yourself and the world.

Khomei can be achieved by producing a long, steady note with an open, relaxed mouth and throat. By altering lip and tongue positions and saying the vowels "ooo", "ohhh", "ahhh", "eee", different Overtones can be produced. Placing your hands over your ears while you do this may help to identify these Overtones initially. Maintain a single tone as you tighten your throat, chest and/or stomach muscles slightly until you find the right spot to produce the Overtone.

If you choke, or start coughing, don't worry, this often happens in the beginning, but you may have to try a different fundamental base note. If you begin coughing, to avoid damage to your vocal chords don't continue to force the sounds out of your throat. Initially, you should be able to make droning sounding vowels, a bit like the droning background hum of bagpipes being played. Now experiment with subtle changes to the position of your tongue, lips, or jaw to create the Overtones. Keep experimenting until you find a spot, or spots where the Overtone notes start to appear. Initially, keep experimenting using subtle changes in muscle tone, and changing shape of your mouth, lips and throat. With time and a lot of patience, different notes can be produced at will, above the steady droning fundamental note that you started with. Eventually, you will be able to produce simple tunes. As you start to create melodies, avoid the temptation to alter the fundamental, because everything will disappear.

In the *sygyt* technique, the throat is tightened to sound an "eee" and the jaw is shifted slightly forward with the mouth almost closed and the lips tightly pursed. The sides of the tongue are pressed up against the upper premolars and molars and the sound is directed between the tongue and palate. Moving the middle of your tongue up and down creates a range of different possible notes. A variation in the style uses the tip of the tongue folded back onto the middle of the palate. Mongolian singers favor of this position.

In the *khoomei-borbangy* technique, the tongue is kept low in the mouth to emphasise the lower, subtler Overtones. The tongue tip is held in a relaxed position at the base of the lower incisors, while gently flexing the middle of the tongue. The jaw is shifted slightly forward and the lips are relaxed as if to pronounce an "ohhh" sound. As the harmonic note appears, you will feel your lips should quiver or tingle slightly. Slightly opening and closing the jaw may help to find the spot where this vibration starts.

Different techniques are used to produce inharmonic Overtones. Overtone singers often refine the Overtones by slightly opening and closing their lips. In Tuva, this style of music is known as *sygyt* ("whistle"). In another technique, singers move their tongues forward and backward, which in normal speech changes the vowel sound from "ohhh" to "eeee" and back again. In the *khoomei* style of singing, two or more pitches may be produced simultaneously.

Other methods change the shape of the throat rather than in the mouth. For low harmonics, singers place the base of the tongue near the rear of the throat. For mid-range harmonics, they move the base of the tongue forward until a gap is produced between the back of the tongue and the soft palate. For the highest harmonics, the soft palate is drawn down over the back of the tongue to divert the breath through the nose. Further refinement of the harmonic notes occurs when slowly widening an narrowing the mouth by flexing the cheek muscles. Tuvinians combine this technique with secondary Overtones in the *kargvraa* style in which very highly pitched harmonics are created.

Getting technical

In practice a Tuvinian singer would sound a fundamental note at a frequency of about 100 hz, and then create a series of harmonic Overtones of this note ranging from the 5th through to the 13th harmonic. This is equivalent to a range of frequencies between 600 and 1,300 Hz. Some of these singers can generate higher harmonics in the range between the 16th and 23rd harmonics, equivalent to tones oscillating between 1,600 and 2,300 Hz, using their nasal cavities as well as their throats.

If the singer sounds a fundamental pitch at 100 Hz, and the first harmonic Overtone occurs at 200 Hz (written H1 = 200 Hz), harmonic two (written H2) will be 400 Hz, H3 = 600 Hz, etc.

In the *sygyt* style of singing, the melody ends with a sustained fundamental on which the singer superimposes a second melody with Overtones using predominantly H9, H10 and H12.

Kargyraa style, is set at a higher pitch, with the fundamental note in the range of 55H to 70 Hz with a range of harmonics from H1 (= 240 Hz) to as high as H12 (= 2880 Hz).The shape of the throat and mouth are changed to vary the range of harmonic note created entirely from a single amplified harmonic of the fundamental note. This note is partly created by altering the flow of air through the mouth and the nose and it usually has a distinctively nasal sound, more like a note sounded on a violin than a flute.

The *borbannadyr* style creates a multiple note effect with the fundamental and the fifth harmonic Overtones creating the base drone, while a second higher Overtone produces the melody. The position of the lips creates and amplifies this Overtone note. This style is sung in a higher pitch than in *kargyraa* with more nasal resonance.

In the Tibetan tradition, the *dbyangs* prayers use vowels as a means of modifying Overtones. Overtone H10 (which is three octaves and a major 3rd above the fundamental) is usually used. The monks start with a mantra based on the word HUM, then change to OM, and then to AH, or another mantra. The bass note which the Gyuto monks chant is two octaves below middle C, vibrating at 75.5 cycles per second. The deepest range of a Western opera singer is in the range of 150 cycles per second, nearly twice as high as the extraordinary bass notes used by these monks. This note therefore may be thought of a sub-harmonic or undertone that is an octave below the fundamental tone. The monks also commonly use an harmonic which is two octaves and a third higher than that bass note (D). The fifth and tenth harmonics are often also created.

The Gyume monks create a different Overtone in their chanting. This harmonic is characteristically two octaves and a 5th higher than their lowest note (F).

HOW TO START DOING IT YOURSELF

AN EASY WAY to start learning the technique is to practice sounding the letters of the alphabet deep down in the throat with your mouth half open and lips slightly apart. Certain notes set up vibrations in the mouth, nose and body. The letter L requires the placement of the tip of the tongue on the palate, causing a resonance through the nose, while other letters, particularly the vowels, set up resonating vibrations lower down in the throat and chest. While initiating these resonating vibrations takes experimentation and careful muscle control, especially if it is intended that they be sounded aloud, the production of these resonances are at the same time very subtle.

A favorite schoolboy trick is to rub the rim of a wine glass (gently and with a slightly moist finger) to set off a resonating, whistle-like hum. People who have tried this will confirm that if the glass rim is rubbed with too much pressure, nothing happens. Similarly if the fingertip is too dry, or the rubbing action too speedy, or there is too much wine left in the glass, it simply won't work. By varying the speed, moisture, pressure etc. until the right combination is achieved, suddenly, and usually without warning, a vibration is felt in the fingertip, and the sound of a single ringing note is heard to emanate from the wine glass. Once the right combination of pressure, speed, moisture etc is achieved, it is easy to reproduce the note almost at will. Until the correct formula is found, it is frustratingly impossible to get any sound from the glass. The same applies to *khoomei*. Experiment with each letter, humming the base note in the throat, but **slowly** and subtly changing the shape of the throat, windpipe, mouth, to change the rate of airflow, and position of the tongue. With practice (and luck), a resonating note at a higher pitch will suddenly appear from nowhere. Often this is accompanied by a slight tingle or vibration in the part that is starting to resonate. When this spot is identified and mastered the resonant sound can be easily produced, almost at will. Then a little experimentation in subtle changes to the position may produce different notes, or even several notes together like the chord played on a musical instrument.

SOME HELPFUL TIPS

KEEP THE BASE note humming in the throat all the time, and do not try to actually sound any other notes to artificially produce the Overtone.

2. Try combining two vowels such as Oh and Ah, Eee and Uuu, oscillating between the two several times in one breath.

3. Slowly move the tip of your tongue up and down to change the airflow from top to bottom of your mouth, or divided between the two. Draw it into a point so that the tip just touches the palate, move it to different spots to change the airflow, increase and decrease the pressure of the tip on the palate, broaden it so that the tip leaves the palate and comes to rest between the back teeth, or part the teeth slightly so that the sides of the tongue can slip in between the teeth. Keep experimenting until you find a spot where you feel a tingle, or a tickling sensation, and that is often getting close to the spot where the Overtones will start to appear. Keep experimenting at or near that spot (even - or more importantly, especially - if it tickles).

4. Try sounding the vowel A (ah), E or O (aw) to create a soft comfortable drone in your lower throat or chest. Now move the tip of your tongue to only just touch the palate behind the front teeth as if pronouncing the letter "L", or "N". If this doesn't work try modifying the shape of the throat or mouth cavity by **slowly** changing from A to O and back again.

5. Try diverting the sound up through your nose and back through your mouth again.

6. Try changing the shape of your lips, slightly parting them, closing them, drawing them backwards into a smile, then forwards so that they are pursed like for a kiss.

7. Make all changes in shape, breath pressure, direction of flow etc. **very slowly** to give enough time for the effect of the change to have its effect.

8. It is often necessary to warm up by singing a few ordinary songs before starting *khoomei*. You may find that your lips and mouth will start to respond more spontaneously with time. The result is a readily produced pulsating Overtone flute like sound.

9. The new sensations in your throat, nose and palate will often induce coughing, or tickling sensations. After a while these organs become more accustomed to this. However, if at any time the coughing or tickling sensations become unbearable. The session should be terminated.

10. As Overtone singing has a deeper spiritual resonance, it is important that your mood, attitude, and your inner soul are all at peace, and "at one" with nature. The sounds that reverberate during this singing, resonate with the ethereal, spiritual body, and it is therefore crucial that one is in tune with, and at one with creation. You simply cannot do this effectively if you are in a temper, late for a meeting, studying for exams and short of sleep, or any other similarly stressed situations.

Each person has a different fundamental or base note or pitch on which their specific harmonic Overtones can be generated. This individually unique fundamental note varies according to the tonal quality of the singer's voice, and each individual has to practice different notes and styles of producing them as described above to find the right formula that works for them. What is important is to recognize that this takes time and practice, so you should not expect to find the formula quickly. As this often takes a considerable amount of time to achieve, and most people who have busy lifestyles cannot devote themselves to this task without significantly impinging on their lives, suitable times have to be found for practicing the technique. Some people have found that good times for this are when one is trapped with nothing to do but to wait patiently. For example, waiting for a delayed flight at an airport, being stuck in a traffic jam, while walking alone in the park, enjoying some peace and quiet on holiday, or other situations in which you have time to kill. From a meditative point of view these situations are far from ideal, but they may serve the purpose if no other alternatives exist.

But now our journey needs to take a different path - maybe there are aspects Western music and ancient traditions, or even modern science that can help us find our elusive goal !

'6'

Singing and humming techniques

SOLFEGE
(ALSO KNOWN AS SOLFEGGIO)

"Doe a deer, a female deer,
Ray, a drop of golden sun,
Me, a name I call myself,
Far, a long, long way to run ..."

From the film: *Mary Poppins*

Solfege has been in existence for many, many years. It originated in the Middle Ages somewhere around the 10th or 11th century AD. Originally it was devised to help monks who had no knowledge of music and no musical training, to learn the melodies of Gregorian chants. This system was developed in the absence of musical instruments to provide the correct pitch and accompaniment. Each note of an octave was assigned a sound that would naturally place the voice of the singer on the scale. The assigned sounds are as follows:- Doh, Ray, Me, Fah, Soh, Lah, Te, Doh. The first and last sounds are the same note, but the second one is an octave higher than the first one. This series of sounds can be superimposed on any musical scale. For example, in the scale of C Major, the sounds would correspond to C, D, E, F, G, A, B, C. In the scale of D Major the corresponding notes would be D, E, F#, G, A, B, C#, D and so on. The fundamental, or base note of any given scale is always Doh and the rest of the scale naturally follows from there. When the teacher or leader indicated the appropriate sound, the novice monks could sound the appropriate note, and the other notes in the scale without any knowledge or ability to read music.

More recently, the system of Solfege has been expanded to enable people to develop a natural pitch for singing and listening to music. By training the ear to recognise pitches based on this system, listeners or students not only develop pitch, but also learn the musical relationships and harmonics between different notes. One of the most common relationships between notes on a scale is known as a Major 3rd. The Major 3rd is the first harmonic of the fundamental. In practice therefore, if Doh is always the base or fundamental note, then Me will always be the equivalent Major 3rd to that note. Similarly, Soh will be the Perfect 5th harmonic of the fundamental, and so on. The ability of performers and composers to instinctively recognise these relationships between notes enables them to change key, improvise, and even change the pitch of melodies spontaneously. Variations of the technique can also be used to develop rhythmic changes so that the performer can practice or evolve different interpretations of the melody without the constraints of having to remember and manipulate the words or notes themselves. Using only the sounds of the notes frees the performer or composer to try different rhythms of the same melody easily and quickly.

Most people, even with a great deal of practice, do not develop what is known as "perfect pitch". This is the ability to spontaneously sound a specific note such as middle C. Most people require the fundamental note that they are trying to produce to be sounded on an instrument, often a piano, or a tuning fork. Once they have tuned themselves to that fundamental note, they are then able to produce the rest of the scale spontaneously using the Solfege technique. It is not unusual for people's pitch to drift and go flat while they are singing, and therefore most people need to sound the fundamental note at regular intervals to ensure that they remain on key.

These facilities were not available to the more primitive singers of Tuva, Mongolia, and Turkey, as well as many other places where harmonic Overtone singing evolved. Thus, in these throat singing or harmonic Overtone singing traditions, the natural resting fundamental note was produced by the singer who then produced harmonics on that note. It is therefore self-evident that each singer would produce a different fundamental note due to his or her individual anatomy and vocal chords. The harmonics that arose in these techniques arose spontaneously and unpredictably, which is why the techniques are so varied and complex. There was therefore, no easy or simple way of developing a scale of notes, as we know them. However, when these harmonic sounds were produced in this way, resonant vibrations occurred within the body that created a very special feeling that was interpreted as being a "in tune" with the natural surroundings and the cosmos.

In the Western tradition, the system of music has been developed to a high level of almost mathematical complexity, producing notes, harmonics, cords, and interweaving melodies that are impossible to produce using intuitive and spontaneous harmonic Overtone techniques of Tuva and elsewhere. Therefore, although the spontaneous reverberations in the body that occur when the right harmonic combination is achieved do not occur so readily in Western music, the richness and melodic interplay of voices and music create an inspirational and often uplifting atmosphere in which participants feel "in tune" with themselves, their community, and a greater reality of life and existence. However, the rich musical traditions of religious liturgy, chants, hymns, and even the Gregorian chants themselves, usually require the trained voices of a choir and musical accompaniment, whether in the form of a single musical instrument or even an orchestra.

The individual, seeking to simply create an atmosphere of peaceful and meditative contemplation, does not have the facilities or the ability for achieving these inspirational heights. Listening to music is often a very effective way of creating the mood, or atmosphere necessary for peaceful contemplation. With the increase in the availability of portable music players, the possibilities for listening to inspirational and mood-altering music have increased enormously. Nevertheless, such electronic wonders are not always readily available when out walking, or going about one's daily business. For someone who is uninitiated into the finesse and nuances of music, and not having the facility to turn on "the stereo" at any convenient time, simply sounding different notes on a scale using the Solfege system and maybe even creating little simple melodies, is often a very effective way of creating an atmosphere conducive to peaceful contemplation.

WESTERN SINGING AND OVERTONE SINGING

IN WESTERN SINGING techniques, three methods are described: glottal fry (or vocal), modal singing (singing from the chest, using the diaphragm for control) and falsetto (singing above the normal range). Classical singing voices use a blend of modal singing and falsetto. Glottal fry is not a technique frequently used, so it is not developed or prized in the West.

In normal speech and song, most of the energy is concentrated at the fundamental frequency, and harmonics are perceived as integral elements of timbre. By contrast, in Overtone singing a single harmonic gains such strength that it is heard as a distinct, whistle-like note. Such harmonics often seem to suddenly appear from nowhere, so they sound disembodied.

Creating Overtones while sounding a note vocally is theoretically quite easy to achieve. If the vowels (ee) or (i) are pronounced diverting some of the escaping breath through the nose, the nasal Overtones can be heard (and can be felt as a slight vibration as well). This effect forms the basis of the Mongolian and Tuvinian Overtone singing technique called *khoomei*.

Essentially, pronouncing a vowel sound creates the fundamental note. Different vowel sounds may produce varied effects. The harmonic Overtones arise spontaneously out of these vowel sounds once they are pronounced in such a way as to create a resonating vibration within the throat and/or mouth and nose.

The mechanics of producing melodic Overtones is interesting in that it deprives the prominent harmonic of its identity. As soon as the harmonic Overtone becomes loud enough to produce the sensation of melody, it can no longer contribute to the tone quality of the instrument or voice, having become a melody-bearing element rather than an enriching timbre-bearing element of the fundamental note. As soon as the throat-singing harmonic becomes audible on its own, it loses the timbre of the human mouth that produced it. It is an harmonic which could theoretically belong to any instrument having the same fundamental frequency as the tone which includes it.

To tune an harmonic, the singer varies the fundamental frequency of the humming drone sound produced by the vocal cords by changing the shape of the throat and mouth, and moving the jaws forward and backward, or changing the shape of the lips from narrow to rounded. These contortions reduce energy loss and feed the resonances back to the vocal chords, amplifying the resonance, and tuning the harmonic note. Singers achieve this tuning by raising or lowering the fundamental note until they hear the desired harmonic resonate at maximum amplitude. Overtone singers also vary the rate and manner in which the vocal cords open and close while producing sounds.

By refining the resonant properties normally used to articulate vowels, vocalists re-position, heighten and sharpen the Overtones to increase the amplification and selectivity of the harmonics that are in tune with the formant peak, while simultaneously reducing the extraneous harmonics. A single Overtone is then produced that takes **precedence over the others.**

'7'

Sounds, music and religions

THE BODY, CHAKRAS AND RELIGION

THE MAJORITY OF spiritual traditions in the world have a common shared belief that the world and indeed the Universe itself were recreated by sound. In the Veda tradition of the Hindus, Brahman is almost synonymous with the "the Word", as in a case of the Judaic and Christian traditions where the world was created by the breath and word (and "intention") of God. The Egyptian god Thot was believed to have created the world by his voice alone and over on the other side of the world; the South American Mayans believed that human beings were created and given life by the Divine Word alone.

It is therefore not surprising that sound is considered to be the most important energy in creation. Not only is it the primary and underlying vibrational energy of the world, but it may potentially be harnessed to move us to expanded awareness and heightened emotional states, as well as to give us a sense of peace and calm. When harnessed correctly it may be used to rectify the disharmonies in us and transform disease and ill ease into health. Not only that, but whether consciously or unconsciously we are aware of it, we are continuously bombarded by sound all time. In city life harmonious sounds of nature are overwhelmed by the dissonant cacophony of the sounds of traffic, sirens, hooters, revving engines, ticking clocks, buzzing and beeping electronic equipment etc. It is no wonder that so many of us find that we can return to a state of harmony when we leave the city and go out into the country to somewhere quiet where we can sit and hear and retune or harmonize ourselves to the sounds and sights of nature around us.

Sounds and science

It seemed to Pythagoras that the eight notes on his scale represented some of fundamental rhythm in the Universe. As a result, eight has been considered a very important, almost magical number. Pythagoras constructed his universal view on his octagonal model. The Chinese Taoists also developed an octagonal philosophy based on eight trigrams, which generated 64 hexagrams that are described in the *I Ching*. Similarly in India the "Noble Eightfold Path", and yoga evolved, based on a progression of eight steps.

More recently, the scientific world has rediscovered the fascinating uniqueness of the number eight. The periodic table, which is a tabulation of all of the elements of matter classifies all of the known elements into eight categories, genetic replication has been found to be based on a system of eights (64 = 8x8), and much of organic molecular geometry is based on octagonal geometric patterns. A very important octagonal formation in carbon chemistry is the tetrahedron, and also the octet, (which is the physical structure formed in Buckminster-Fuller "Bucky balls"), and benzene rings (which form the basic physical structure of molecules in many household products in daily use and nature).

Sounds may compliment and amplify each other, creating harmony, or they may clash with each other, creating dissonance. Sometimes they may clash to such an extent that they cancel each other out creating silence.

Every particle in the Universe is in a constant state of movement. This is most obviously observed in the movement of the sun, the moon and the planets. On an atomic level, electrons spin around the nucleus, and indeed, spin around their own axes, in much the same way as the Earth spins around its own axis. This spinning of particles creates rhythms or vibrations that are characteristic for each particle. Particles close to one another interact with each other, and their natural vibrations interact with one another, harmonizing or creating dissonance. So it is that every object in the Universe has a natural vibration or pulse. This applies to our own bodies. Every particle in our bodies has its own pulse of life. We are aware of some of these vibrations, for example, our heartbeats.

We also interact with the vibrations that are around us. The most easily perceived vibrations are sound, and we are surrounded by sounds. Some sounds irritate us (create dissonance) while others please us (create harmony). Therefore, different sounds may completely change our mental and physical states of being. We consciously choose to do this when we listen to music that may please, calm, or stimulate us. We also interact with many sounds around us that we are not even conscious of. When the background noise of our cities irritates us sufficiently, we need to get away, and usually we choose to leave the city for the country. Here we find ourselves enveloped in other waves of sound such as the sounds of the forests, the insects, the wind. And … we feel better for it! The harmonious sounds of the country help us to return to the harmonious state that our bodies and minds need to counterbalance the constant dissonant racket of the city. In Eastern philosophies it is believed that these natural harmonious sounds promote our well-being. They are actually necessary to keep "our batteries charged" (that is, our sense of well being, our vitality, our feelings of harmony with our surroundings).

Chakras

Every cell, and organ in our bodies has its own specific pulse or vibration, the essence of achieving and maintaining both physical, emotional and spiritual health is to achieve and maintain an harmonious relationship among all of the parts of the body, and also with the external environment of our homes, our work, our communities, cities, etc., etc. In Eastern philosophies, we not only have our own internal natural vibrations with their harmonious Overtones that are unique to each one of us, and which change as a reflection of our moods, our state of health etc, but we also create a small pulsating fields around us. This field of vibratory energy is known as an "aura". The aura is generated by the electro-magnetic fields that we (and everything else) generate because we are made up of vibrating atoms that are electrically charged. The constant movement of all of the particles of nature creates interactive magnetic fields. Each chakra represents an area of concentration of our electromagnetic fields or auras. These energy points are specific for each part of our bodies and they are considered to be an essential part of the physical body, though not physically obvious. Each chakra reflects the state of the related part of the physical body and conversely, the physical body reflects the state of the aura and the chakras.

Chakras concentrate points of manifestation for energy emanating from the physical body. From the chakras, the energy is thought to condense into physical acupuncture points, then, condensing further, this energy diffuses to become part of the physical body. In most esoteric traditions, there are seven major chakras that are centrally located along the front of the body. They are the keys to the area of the physical body where they are located. Many physical imbalances may be perceived as being the result of imbalanced chakras. The following is a short summary of the chakras:

1. **The base chakra** (in Sanskrit, *muladhar*) is located at the base of the spine and is also associated with the anus. This chakra is related to the adrenal glands and associated with issues of survival.

2. **The sacral chakra** (in Sanskrit, *svadhishthana*) is located three to five centimeters below the navel. This chakra is related to the sexual organs and reproductive function.

3.   **The navel chakra** (in Sanskrit, *manipura*) is located around the navel. This chakra is associated with the digestive organs. It is often thought of as the chakra from which our power and mastery of self originates.

4.   **The heart chakra** (in Sanskrit, *anahata*) is located in the centre of the chest between the two nipples. It is associated with the organs of the heart and respiration as well as the thymus gland. This is the chakra of love and compassion.

5.   **The throat chakra** (in Sanskrit, *vishuddi*) is located in the throat. It is associated with speech and hearing and with the thyroid gland. It is the chakra of communication and creativity.

6.   **The brow chakra** (in Sanskrit, *ajna*) is often referred to as "the third eye" and is located between the eyebrows. This is the energy centre often referred to as the third eye.

This chakra is associated with imagination, psychic and spiritual matters. Some traditions consider this chakra to be associated with the secretary functions of the master gland of the endocrine system, the pituitary gland, but this is not universally accepted.

The crown chakra (in Sanskrit, *sahasrara*) is located at the top of the head. It is said to control every aspect of the body and mind and is associated with full enlightenment and union with God and the Universe. There is some confusion as to whether this energy centre controls the pituitary or the pineal gland. This chakra is seldom opened except in cases of the most adept practitioners of meditative arts.

The sounds of the chakra centers

Hello darkness my old friend,
I've come to talk to you again,
Because a vision softly increeping…

Simon & Garfunkel

Root (base of Spine): LAM: Ohhhh
Sacrum: VAM: Shuuuuuuu
Solar RAM: Yaaaaaaa
Heart YAM: Waaaaaa
Throat: HAM: Heeeeee
Brow: OM: Huuuuuuu
Crown (of head): Ieeeeeeee

This short introduction to the chakras should be supplemented by further reading on the subject, and it is important to emphasise that this is only a very general overview of the chakra system.

Different traditions place different attributes on specific centers, and associate chakra centers with different sets of glands and organs. From the point of view of this book however, it is important only to appreciate that there are centers of concentration of energy that are in direct harmony or disharmony with underlying parts of the underlying physical body, and can be used to tune the physical body to its optimal state of health and well being. Each of the chakra centers is said to resonate to different sound frequencies (or vibrations). A number of different systems have evolved using sound to resonate with the chakra points. In some cases, even different sounds and meditations are used. All of these work, because each person is slightly different, and what works for one person does not necessarily work for another. Exploring different techniques and possibilities are often the only way to focus and tune the energies of the system to their optimal level.

Most commonly though, by aligning and balancing a chakra centre with an afflicted organ it can become healthy and the problem may resolve itself. As they are activated, the individual opening these chakras seems to achieve a raised level of consciousness and spiritual awareness. This energizing of the vitality, known in the East as *kundalini* (Indian) or *chi* (Chinese) that is said to sleep in the base chakra, awakens the energy of the chakra centres. The *kundalini* energy is directed up the spine to the next chakra progressively until it reaches the crown (i.e. the head), where the individual becomes fully awakened and spiritually conscious. With the raising of the *kundalini* energy, and the activation of succeeding chakras, different powers and abilities become manifest. Sound is considered to have the crucial ability of enabling an individual to awaken their *kundalini* energy.

Vowel sounds create a resonance in the physical body. Vowels may form the essential vibratory energy to awaken the *kundalini*, but they may also act as the fundamental note for the production of harmonic Overtones. Particular harmonics (also called formants) are generated with specific vowels. While every vowel can create every harmonic in a scale, each vowel has a particular set of harmonics that are amplified. By using vowel sounds as mantras, individuals may start to create awakening Overtones without any formal training.

There seems to be a direct relationship between the pitch of the note, and the chakra. The lower chakras are in tune with lower notes and the upper chakras in tune with by higher notes. There also appears to be a direct relationship between specific vowels and different parts of the body.

These vowel sounds seem to work independently to resonate the chakra centers. Such resonation techniques are said to be very old. Therefore, sounding vowel sounds combined with pitch alterations, initiates very powerful sonic formulae for resonating both the physical and spiritual body through the subtle energy centers.

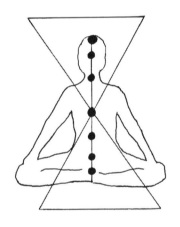

Awakening the Chakra centers is based on the intonation of a number of primary syllables known as *bija*. These are a bit like the Eastern equivalent of Solfege. The *bija* are, transcending from the lowest to the highest physical and spiritual levels, LUNG, VANG, RAM, UNG, HUNG, OM, AH. By simply sounding these words and prolonging their intonation, it is apparent that their reliance on the vowels, and the ending "ng" creates different indefinable harmonic resonances ascending from the very relaxed and easy to pronounce VANG, through to HUNG which requires a tautening of the cheek and chest muscles and the lips to pronounce, through to the higher chakra sounds.

The Chakras are made up of orbs, or centers of spiritual energy progressing from the purely physical at the base of the spine up to the purely ethereal at the crown of the head. As in the Hebraic tradition there are direct resonances, using mantric formulae between parts of the physical body and equivalent parts of the cosmic body. In the same way as resonant spiritual contemplations start at the most basic physical level (the base of the spine in the Hindu system, or the roots of the tree in the Kabalistic system) and progress upwards to the higher levels of ethereal contemplation, transcending the physical body in the process, each Chakra (Hindu) or Sefir (Kabbalah) has to be tuned and mastered before proceeding into the next and higher level.

Jewish Traditions

Most ancient traditions refer to the word or the breath or the sound of the Creator of the Universe. In the Jewish tradition there are a number of references to sound and its powerful properties. In the Torah (the five books of Moses forming the basis of the Bible), there is the famous story of the blowing of the trumpets causing the walls of Jericho to come tumbling down. In addition, the ancient Hebrew name for God may not be pronounced because the sound of it is considered to be so powerful that unpredictable forces might be unleashed in saying it. These statements are deep echoes of very powerful ancient beliefs in the power of primordial sounds. The sounds could not only affect objects and matter, but could move them or destroy them. Each

letter of the Hebrew alphabet is considered to have a unique resonance with Creation, and sounding single letters, words or groups of words may have especially powerful resonances that reverberate into the cosmos.

The Hebrew mystical tradition is known as Kabbalah. In this tradition the Universe is likened to a "Tree of Life" with an ascent from the physical world (in the roots of the Earth) to the hidden or metaphysical world (via the trunk and through its branches to its highest pinnacles). On the tree are ten Sephirot (orbs of concentrated metaphysical energy of the Divine Presence). These orbs or "centers of wisdom" are each associated with a different level of reality and consciousness, so each one has specific physical and metaphysical characteristics including colour, and most importantly, sound. Therefore, by sounding the correct note for each orb or harmonic of it, it might be possible to achieve resonance with that orb and its attributes. It is believed that the essential sounds, or frequencies and rhythms necessary to achieve this resonance were part of the secret knowledge held by the Levi's (who were the ancient tribe of Israel who formed the functionaries of the Temple). Although the knowledge of the sounds associated with invoking the powers of the Sephirot ("centers of wisdom") have in effect been lost with the destruction of the Temple in Jerusalem and the dispersal of the tribes of Israel, some work has been undertaken in modern times overlaying the sounds associated with the chakras with those of a Kabalistic tree.

The harmonic sounds link each letter to different "vibrations" or "emanations" with the cosmos and metaphysical existence. So important is this concept that Jews may not pronounce the name of God because the very name, if pronounced correctly, could cause such powerful resonances that it might invoke overwhelming forces emanating from the Deity. Kabalistic Judaism, which is the mystical tradition of Judaism, has developed a system of contemplation based on the tree of life. In

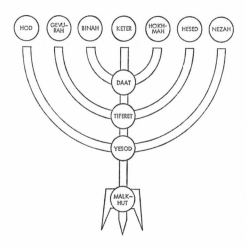

this tree of life there are ten Sefirot (singular is Sefir), or orbs (or balls of energy), each reverberating with its own specific colour and sound.

The Kabalistic tree is a highly complex system of geometric patterns of interconnections between resonating centers of the physical body and the spiritual body and the cosmos. The sound progression is not the same as in the *bija*, but it progresses from a humming "mm" through the mother letters described previously V, H, and Y, ending in "sh". Although the actual letters used, and therefore the sounds produced, are different in the two systems, the progression is from the relaxed hum of the "m" sound through more complex sounds ending in the sound of carefully controlled rushing air, "sh". In ascending the Kabalistic tree, this sequence of sounds is repeatedly intoned at increasingly higher pitches progressing from the physical through to the higher levels of consciousness and beyond.

The opening, or awakening, or tuning in, to the resonant centres of the Kabalistic tree and dwelling on them to refine the harmonic vibrations creates a purity of resonant sound which facilitates spiritual enlightenment at different levels and planes. In the same way as emotions and feelings can be conveyed not simply by communicating using language, but by overlying the words with emotional intonations, so too can the harmonic reverberations activate the centers of spiritual or psychic energy to become the conduits for the interaction of physical and metaphysical beings. This has developed into a fine art in most religious traditions with the intonation of certain vowel sounds associated with specific resonances are not only used extensively, but when combined musically or in the form of chanting, with the possible addition of repetitive drum beating, or inspirational melodies enhances, amplifies and focuses key harmonics designed to be opened in communal prayer. This may be further enhanced by the use of body movements. In some traditions the use of ritual and sacred dances are an integral part of communal prayer. This is characteristically not part of the Hebraic and Western traditions, but in some Jewish communities it is customary to sway or rock the body rhythmically during the intonation or chanting of certain prayers. This serves to physically create a union between the words, the rhythm of the poetic form of the prayer and the chant.

Christian traditions

In the Christian tradition it is written: *In the Beginning was the Word, and the Word was with God, and the Word was God'* (John 1:1). 'The Word' quite clearly refers to sound, which is the God-force or creative force of the Universe. In the Hindu tradition the word AUM, which many of us know as OM, was the sound that called the Universe into being.

Even in modern day society, the ultimate in sound is described in the 'Big Bang' theory of creation, which must be the loudest of all the sounds imaginable. In fact, it is modern Western science that provides the most convincing evidence of the power of sound to shape and transform matter. High frequency sound is used extensively in industry, medicine and dentistry for cleaning, dislodging, and disrupting adherent materials, usually in the form of ultrasonic vibrations. Harnessing the power of sound can therefore be used as the basis of the healing potential of sound.

The power of sound

Therefore, in summary, not only the words, but the music and the rhythm of meditation, contemplation, and prayer form an integral and essential part of attempting to approach the greater ethereal essence of the Universe, that many of us call God. The use of melody and chanting activate and focus predominantly on the realms of the heart and head (i.e. chakras or sephirot), which are the essential aspects of the physical body involved in prayer, as opposed, maybe, to other centers such as the limbs, which predominate during physical work and exercise. In chanting, the words are charged or activated by the harmonic resonances that energize the body to harmonic movement, and the mind to shift its psychological and spiritual state.

Often the communal harmonization of key sounds or notes is the setting stage for then honing and tuning those and maybe other, harmonic vibrations on an individual level through inner, personal exploration as opposed to communal ritual. Meditating or contemplating key harmonic sounds while sitting still in a comfortable armchair almost inevitably leads to sleep. Performing exactly the same contemplative techniques while walking in the beauty of a natural setting, rocking or swaying the body, or combined with other physical activities such as breathing or stretching (as in yoga, t'ai chi, and others) enhances and

complements the inter-relationships of the physical and psychic bodies, and helps to avoid failure in attempting to achieve spiritual peace and solace by conscious intention alone.

Primordial speech and resonances

At a more fundamental level, sounds can also be used for healing purposes and for transformation of people's lives by establishing an harmonic resonance with the powerful forces of godliness that pervade the Universe. Sound therefore, in effect, is thought to be a conduit between the physical and metaphysical dimensions.

As people began to make sounds and communicate, three primordial sounds formed the basic foundations for building language: "ohhh", "eeee", and "aahhh". These are thought to have been the first differentiated sounds emitted by human beings. In order to utter the sounds, it was necessary to change the shape and position of the lips and mouth creating expressions to go with the sounds. Thus it was that communication began. The ultimate communication (i.e. with the primary forces of the Universe) was therefore based on these three sounds. Establishing an harmonic resonance with the metaphysical planes of existence would create what is referred to in many texts as "sacred sounds".

In the Jewish tradition, the name of God was only intoned by the High Priest, only on the holiest day of the year (Yom Kippur), after which the assembled congregation intoned ... Amen. It should be noted that it was specified that the Amen should be intoned so as to linger on the last letter, in other words, Amennnnnnnnnnnnnnnnn. This would tend to create a tonal vibration after the intonation of the ineffable name by the High Priest. Lingering on a single letter/note such as the "n", is almost akin to humming, creating harmonic vibrations within the body and the mind in a way that has the potential to create or concentrate altered states of perception, or altered physical and mental states.

Similarly, the use of resonant sounds such as "oommm" in the Buddhist tradition, and sacred and chants for balancing the Chakras are well established in Eastern traditions.

But much of our journey has been into the past; let's now explore the present.

'8'

Sound therapy

SOUND THERAPY IS based on the principle of "sympathetic harmony" which is also known as "sympathetic resonance". Resonance is the frequency of vibration of an object. Sympathetic resonance occurs when one vibrating object causes another to vibrate in harmony with it. By creating vibrations in the form of sound, with Overtones that amplify each other in tune with some other object, vibrations may be induced in those objects. This is the way in which singers are supposed to be able to break glasses with their voices.

Each part of the body, must have its optimum, *healthy* frequency, or rate of vibration and be in harmony with its neighbors. When we are ill, it is because some part of us is not vibrating harmoniously (i.e. creating dissonance) within itself, or with the other parts of our bodies, or with our surroundings. This dissonance, or illness, may be healed restoring the affected parts to their natural healthy frequencies. One of the best ways of achieving this is with sound, tuned to achieve sympathetic resonance with the unwell part of the body.

HEALTH AND SOUND THERAPY

MUSIC IS AMAZING! Whether in the form of song or dance, complex concertos or simple tunes, rhythmic drumming or sacred chants, listening or performing, music has the ability to change our emotions, to ease our daily stresses, to give us strength and vitality, and to inspire us to greatness. In so many ways music can influence our well-being, or help us return to a state of wellness. The use of play-acting, communal singing and dancing and rhythmic games in children's groups and schools are well known ways of helping to develop social skills, confidence, and emotional expression. More sophisticated applications of these "creative play" sessions based on musical expression in a non-threatening pleasant environment apply equally effectively to adults.

Sound healers of antiquity, in which category I include shamans, *sangomas*, certain monks, and anyone who regularly uses sound to feel better, or to help others feel better, have many tools at their disposal. Western sound therapists use a combination of voice, acoustic devices and sacred instruments from different cultures. An intimate working knowledge of sound, intention, intuition and energy, if applied correctly, can potentially effect powerful changes on every level of one's being. The use of sound is therefore an holistic therapy operating on physical, emotional, mental and spiritual levels.

THERAPEUTIC USES OF OVERTONE CHANTS

ONE OF THE most powerful forms of sound healing is the ancient technique of Overtone chanting. Its origins lie in central Asia where shamans of the Turkic races of Mongolia and Tuva have practiced it for centuries. In South Africa it is practiced by Xhosa women, and in Tibet it is used exclusively by the Llamas. It has also become a beautiful form of musical expression. Known *as khoomei* in Asia, *nwokolo* by the Xhosa, and as Overtone chant or vocal harmonics in the West. It allows a single person to sing two, three, or even four simultaneous sounds.

By means of focused intention and thought direction, and employing as many resonators as possible within the body and cranium, one can amplify and manipulate the harmonics (the partial tones of which the voice is made) or Overtones of the fundamental tone being sung. These Overtones are perceived as clear, flute-like or bell-like tones above the lower drone of the voice.

The Tibetan Buddhist path to self-realization involves the understanding of the Three Mysteries. These are the Mysteries of Body, Speech and Mind, whose experience has been condensed into the mantric formula OM-AH-HUM. Speech is the link between the Mind (ethereal) and the Body (physical). Speech is the understanding of sound as the creative force and incorporates the knowledge of using a mantra as a sacred tool for summoning up the appearance of gods and the forces of the Universe. Through the creation of several tones at the same time, the "One-Voice Chord" may be a further condensation of the Three Mysteries into an expression of Body, Speech and Mind as pure tone.

The religious chanting of the Tibetan monks creates a second hum usually in the throat, which is then amplified, resulting in as many as four simultaneous Overtones. The droning fundamental note works mainly on the physical body by setting up predominantly physical vibrations within it, while the Overtones work mainly on the ethereal, metaphysical or spiritual body. In addition to acoustic instruments often used to accompany the chanting, the human voice has a unique characteristic: it conveys and transmits intention, will, sentiments and emotions. It is possible for most people to sense the mood of another simply by listening to the subtle nuances, changes in tone, and rhythm while they are talking. This non-verbal communication is concentrated and therefore magnified in Overtone singing or chanting.

HOW SOUND HEALS

USING SOUND FOR healing stems from the belief that when our natural resonance is disturbed, (i.e. out of harmony), we can return to harmony, (i.e. retune to health), by deliberately reintroducing the appropriate energy, as sound, into our bodies, or our immediate surroundings. Sound can break up patterns or introduce new ones. The technique of sound healing is therefore based on establishing resonant tones that retune the fields or infuse the body with waves of sound energy eliminating the dissonant eddy currents that are the source of illness.

MUSIC THERAPISTS

MODERN MUSIC THERAPISTS exploit these characteristics of music to help people return to a state of wellness. They work in a wide range of environments from hospitals, day-care centers, rehabilitation centers, and schools, to old-age homes and with specific groups with specific needs. They work with all age groups from small children or to the elderly - with groups, families and even individuals.

Generally speaking, music therapists aim to help individuals with physical and/or emotional problems, those with social and communication difficulties, and others whose cognitive skills are damaged as result of developmental and learning disabilities or trauma and age-related conditions such as Alzheimer's disease. Depending on the needs of the group, specific music sessions are prescribed. Sessions may include anything from singing, dancing, writing music or lyrics, performing music, listening to music or discussing it and criticizing aspects of music. Music may also sometimes be used to enhance its imagery and spirituality, or as a way of facilitating inner peace (i.e. tuning in), or external peace with family, friends, work stresses, community, etc.

The influence of music on human beings has been known since time immemorial. The ancient shamans and tribal witch doctors were well versed in using repetitive rhythm, and simple tunes to create hypnotic states, heightened awareness, and to "receive communications" from their deities. Formalized and complex music, commissioned and performed mainly in churches and cathedrals, have long been used to create inspirational and spiritually enhanced states during prayer.

In recent times musicians were invited into institutions and hospitals to perform for inmates or to create a pleasant diversion for them. With time it was recognised that careful choice of the music and dances could have specific therapeutic benefits, and the concept of music therapy was born. Today, degree courses exist in music therapy, as well as a number of sophisticated journals devoted to music therapy. Music has also become an integral part of our lives on an informal basis, where it is used in shopping malls, restaurants, hospitals and our homes as a background accompaniment to our lives, creating a relaxed, almost subliminal, background ambience. In some situations such as during exercise it is used as an accompaniment to stimulate better performance. Many of us simply use music passively to encourage and enhance or relaxation.

It is claimed that music therapy can improve communication skills, improve academic performance, improve motor skills (e.g. learning to play an instrument), strengthen social and leisure skills, and decrease anti-social behavior, stress reduction and pain management. Some music therapists specialize in helping individuals in their personal growth and development. To this end any number of untrained "therapists" or "guides" have produced musical recordings that are extensively marketed to encourage altered states of awareness, focused thought, and spiritual development. Protagonists of the use of music in this way believe that music may influence our emotions and our feelings of well-being, but rarely is it focused in such a way as to influence our deeper consciousness, and indeed our natural body functions and rhythms. In these techniques music conjures up feelings or visible images and sometimes even basic physiological changes such as sweating, changes in breathing and heart rate, muscle relaxation, or even involuntary muscle activity such as tapping in time to music.

CAN SOUND HEAL?

THE COMBINATION OF music and imagery is a powerful means of guiding the consciousness. This is well developed in a religious context in the creation of images, for example, stained glass windows in churches and cathedrals, together with the use of inspirational and uplifting music. In Eastern traditions, the combination of staring at a fixed object or Mandala while intoning a mantra or other sounds is also well established. Dr Helen Bonny, a music therapist in the United States has developed a technique called "guided imagery and music" in which carefully selected evocative music is played in a comfortable relaxed environment to bring to the surface deep-seated images, emotions, sensations and dreamlike symbols which can then be used as therapeutic and/or educational tools. More importantly though, specific sounds are embedded in our memories and are often associated with specific occurrences or emotional experiences in our lives.

On one hand, replaying these sounds may evoke past memories and emotions, but on the other hand, during states of altered consciousness or heightened awareness, our perception of the sounds around us changes, so as to proactively communicate (or resonate) with parts of our minds and bodies that are normally inaccessible. The experiences evoked by the music may be negative (relating to bad experiences or emotions) or positive (relating to feelings of well-being and heightened spirituality). The guide, or therapist's role is in dealing with the negative experiences as part of a therapeutic team that might include social workers, psychiatrists, and others. Similarly, guiding the listener through the labyrinth of positive experiences, which may result in extreme experiences of over stimulation, might also have to be dealt with. It is said by some that these techniques reach the creative unconsciousness in the deeper conscious self, opening imagery that facilitates new insights into our minds and bodies. In a way this can be likened to enhanced and focused daydreams, in which the mind is guided through its natural tendency to wander into its own world by the use of music.

More recent variations on these techniques have included the development of focused psychoanalytic tools in which the use of carefully selected music and sets of defined images are designed to elicit responses from clients undergoing therapy. Evoking the specific images and feelings, which are unique to each client, would then act as the basis for psychotherapy.

In some schools of music therapy the use of simple vowel "toning" has been advocated as a way of encouraging the body to achieve harmony, relieve stress, and reach a state of well-being. Vowel toning is a simple technique in which vowels are sounded and maintained for an extended period of time to enable them to resonate with the body. These physical vibrations not only encourage the natural physiological rhythms of the body to harmonize, but tune into and synchronize to the natural rhythms of the brain creating a sense of physical and emotional health. Prolonging the intonation of a specific vowel enables the body to harmonize and vibrate in tune with it, which does not happen if the same vowel is sounded during speech, or even singing. Different vowels may have different resonances within the body, and as each person's voice is different, producing unique harmonic Overtones, the vowels that set up the best resonances may be different for each person.

'9'

Sound today

NEW AGE MUSIC AND THERAPY

THE TECHNIQUES OF music therapy have been adapted and freely marketed within the New-Age community. Any number of "mind and body" workshops exist to explore the "vibrational resonances" of sounds and music to promote health and healing and general well-being. The music chosen is said to set up powerful resonances within the listener to promote healing by resonating and developing their positive and health-promoting aspects. In addition, it can be used to improve the quality of life and develop positive attitudes in a non-threatening relaxed way, contributing to personal growth and development. For these reasons the use of sounds, music, incantations, and harmonic singing for this purpose has come to be termed "holistic healing" and is often combined with other techniques such as dancing or art forms to achieve wellness.

Many have found playing or listening to carefully selected music, is a more satisfying and in many ways more effective way of achieving altered conscious states, heightened awareness and spiritual growth than the use of "designer drugs", so popular among many of our communities today. Indeed, music often forms an integral part of the therapy aimed at rehabilitating drug abusers. On a lesser level, literally hundreds of self-help groups have been formed using drumming, flute playing, chimes and string instruments, rhythmic chanting and/or dancing to achieve these states of well-being. While these groups are by and large useful for team building and mutual support by sharing of mutual experiences, and for achieving harmonious relationships with others in the group, these groups cannot help the individual on the arduous introspective path of personal expansion.

HIGH-TECH SOLUTIONS

THE USE OF pure sound to cure physical ailments has also become popular. Several systems exist to potentiate healing using high tech machinery.

"Cymatic" therapy, as it is called, uses computer generated sounds within the auditory range that are applied to the surface of the body to transmit resonant frequencies of sound into the body. According to this therapy, each organ and tissue making up the body has an "harmonic factor" (called the H-factor), so that signals from a machine are designed to specifically synchronize with the highly specific H-factors for the tissue or part of the body being treated. No claims are made for any curative properties, but treatment is said to reduce the need for drugs, reduce pain and to promote faster healing in sufferers.

Other ways of using sound and sound waves to achieve altered perception and different states of consciousness have also used technology to change patterns of brain activity. For example, the Monroe Institute in the USA has produced a series of audiotapes, which it claims induce relaxed and meditative states. This is achieved by altering the brain patterns of electrical activity in different parts of the brain. By choosing the appropriate tape (e.g. relaxation, or stimulation) different brain wave patterns can be amplified. Stimulating the specific brain "waves" such as **alpha** (daydreams, heightened awareness and inspiration), **beta** (physical activity), **delta** (sleeping and relaxation), and **theta** (meditative states), the appropriate part of the brain can be energized and focused to achieve the optimum state of consciousness or altered consciousness being sought.

The tapes use a combination of repetitive beating, pure sound and occasionally some words to harmonize with the appropriate brainwaves or combination of brainwaves and focus them. Stereophonic headphones are used to listen to the sounds that are slightly different for each ear. This audio system is called

Hemi Sync These tapes are by no means unique, and many similar systems based on Tibetan chanting, Tuvinian Overtone throat singing, drumming, white sound, mantras and many others exist and are actively marketed and reputed to achieve similar results.

You can even try out one of these systems for free on the internet. Go to www.bwgen.com (bwgen stands for "brainwave generator") and try it out. You do need to plug headphones into your computer, because simply listening to the sounds through the speakers doesn't work!

Meditative sounds of silence

... and the words of the prophet are written on the subway walls,
And tenement halls,
And whispered in the sounds of silence ...
Simon & Garfunkel

An alternative system is described as ELF (Extremely Low Frequency), in which "meditation goggles" produce rhythmically flashing lights in combination with headphones emitting low frequency (4-13 cycles per second) "phase-shifted" sound. It is claimed that this combination of light and sound influence **alpha** and **theta** brainwaves to produce specific altered states of consciousness. It is also claimed that using this unit, anything from improved memory to out-of-body and paranormal experiences can be achieved in only a few weeks!

Another system called a "neurophone" claims that it bypasses normal audio perception, by passing information through the skin, directly to the brain. The device has electrodes that are placed on the head or face and any form of sound can be inputted into it. Whether music or factual information, it is claimed that anything from telepathy to accelerated learning can be achieved. Some purveyors of these machines and their agents have actually claimed that they are able to use resonating sound at specific low frequency ranges to alter the intentions and emotions, or even disable the neural systems of others, remotely. There are even claims made (and vehemently denied), that the USA, as well as other countries, possess and use radio frequency weapons used to transmit sounds and subliminal messages to the enemy and alter their bellicose battle plans.

Many other "brainwave" altering machines and devices for relaxation, altered perception and even astral projection have been developed, and are freely available. These devices are all based on the use of of sound. Sometimes music, or the sounds of nature are used to create altered states of consciousness. Not infrequently "white sound," or "silent sound" are used. These sounds, which often sound remarkably like the fundamental buzzing notes produced by Tuvinian and other harmonic Overtone singers, act in the same way by creating a resonating note that harmonizes with the natural rhythms and electrical fields of the body, and particularly the brain.

Disease may be considered to be a vibrational disharmony within the body. If that is so, sound resonance with the use of Overtone/harmonic chanting can bring the body back into harmony and thus heal the person. As a biological feedback element, *khoomei* has many advantages over other methods. It is portable and needs no external power source, it is invisible and can be as private or as public as the individual desires.

Sound has both healing potential and the ability to do harm. Its power and effects are all pervading. Consider some facts: Sound is energy. Sound can be used to heat objects or shatter them (e.g. ultrasonic energy).

Sound creates form. Sound can induce characteristic patterns and waves when applied to liquid or semi-liquid substances as seen if a vibrating object such as a vibrating tuning fork is placed in a bowl of water.

Sound can carry intention, emotion and feelings. For example, we can interpret emotions, sense danger, anger disapproval, sadness, disapproval etc by simply listening to people's voices.

WHAT KIND OF MUSIC TURNS YOU ON?

THE YEARNING FOR a better quality of life and personal growth and development in a spiritual sense has increasingly led to the use of carefully chosen music to stimulate, sensitize and energize the psyche. The problem of for most individuals is the "carefully chosen" pieces of music to listen to. There is a substantial industry that has developed, producing and marketing music for this purpose on tapes and CD's. Choice among these New Age and personal development musical compositions is enormous, creating within itself a problem of what to choose or even from whom to seek advice as to the most appropriate music to listen to, or what instrument to play, or what songs to sing.

So how do you find the music that is best for you? This is not at all easy, given the rich and varied musical styles and compositions that are at our fingertips. Maybe a good place to start is by thinking about music. Are there times, places, events or other important occasions at which certain pieces of music were played? ... Or maybe at times of particular happiness that you associate with special music or sounds? ... or are there musical passages that conjure up special images or feelings (particularly good feelings) when you listen to them?

Music with different tempos is important because those with a racy fast tempo stimulate us to action and activity, while those with the slow ponderous tempo stimulate thought and emotion, while those with a light regular rhythm facilitate relaxation. Depending on the mood or feelings that you would like to encourage, you might need to explore a little to find the right type and tempo of music for the right occasion for you.

But how you listen to the music itself is also important. Sit comfortably, where you are not likely to be disturbed. As you listen to the music, try and follow its flow, maybe gently breathing in time with it or even quietly humming the melody, but most importantly think about what images it creates in your mind. Let your mind wander and daydream a little, but if it wanders into parts that you are trying to avoid, bring it back into line with the music. For example, you may need to change your daydream about solving problems at work while listening to a piece of music that you have chosen to harmonize with nature. If you are tense, it may be a good idea to gently flex and relax your muscles rhythmically in time with the music. Starting at your feet and legs, and slowly working up through your body and finally ending with relaxing them all and letting go! Some people find it more effective to either rhythmically sway or rock their bodies, or walk or dance, or even have a physical workout in time to music to achieve this physical release of tension. Actually evolving your own songs and tunes are among the most creative things that the mind can do, and some people have had profoundly emotional experiences while writing songs or creating or playing or singing music, particularly when these are inspired by major life events.

'10'

And finally ...
"do it yourself"!

I'd like to teach the world to sing
In perfect harmony

I'd like to build the world a home
And furnish it with love
Grow apple trees and honey bees and snow-white turtle doves
The New Seekers

Sound has to be transmitted from its source to its sensors. Generally the sensor is the ear, which is specifically adapted to hear the multitude of sounds that surround us. However, we can also feel sound in the form of vibrations in the speakers of a sound system, or the floorboards on which speakers or musical instruments are standing while there are producing sound. Occasionally we might see pictures or other objects starting to vibrate when certain notes are sounded. This secondary sound, produced by setting up vibrations in other objects by the pure transmission of sound is known as resonance. This principle is applied in sonic healing techniques. If some part of the body is diseased or malfunctioning it may be considered to be out of tune, or out of harmony with the rest of the body. By applying the right tone of sound, with the right oscillating frequency and rhythm, it is believed that the disharmonious organ or part can be brought back into harmony creating a healthy state. By harmonizing the affected organ or part with the rest of the body, the whole body re-establishes an harmonious interrelationship and becomes a healthy unit. Not only must the sound be applied at the right tone and frequency, it also it needs to be directed to the part that is no longer in harmony. As this is often an internal part of the body, the sound is transmitted through the tissues by resonance. Although there are several machines designed to treat disease in this way and practitioners of sound therapy use them extensively, there is another aspect of sonic healing that cannot be transmitted by these instruments.

In ancient times it was believed that the sound waves generated by sacred sounds acted as a carrier wave for conscious "intention" in much the same way as carrier radio waves carry the pictures and images for television. Therefore, using sacred sounds to generate these carrier waves, participants are able to transmit their "intentions" to the forces, energies, or powers that surround us, which are able to put them into effect. Whether the Aborigines of Australia using rituals to invoke parts of nature for a good life, or the witch doctors of Africa to cure a disease or the misfortunes of their group, or the native Americans to attain harmony with nature, or the ancient mystical schools of Greece and the Middle East using sound to perform physical feats like destroying the walls of Jericho, or to obtain insight into the future using oracles, the underlying principle was this active use of conscious intention to influence the present and future.

If sound has the ability to transmit "intention", then, if it is the intention of one who is diseased to get well, the intention to do so may be overlaid on the right sonic pattern of tones, harmonies and frequencies, resulting in health. Similarly, if the therapist creating the sound, has the "intention" of creating a healing state in the person being treated, they may get well again if the right harmonies, particularly in the disharmonious parts of the body, can be harmonized. It is thought that the healer not only creates the right sounds and frequencies to resonate with the diseased part of the person being treated, but also creates the right resonances to invoke universal or divine energy through his or her will and "intention" to actively create a healing situation in the region being focused upon. In addition, because we are all unique creations we all naturally oscillate at our own unique frequency. This frequency is usually closely aligned to the natural frequencies of nature, but may, for a variety of reasons, drift further away from normal range of natural frequencies. Retuning, or bringing the natural frequencies of the body and mind back into line is the purpose of sonic healing.

While musical instruments, and those adepts who can lead groups in harmonic Overtone singing and chanting, and even scientific machines that are becoming available (e.g. cymatic instruments or generators), can refocus and harmonize these frequencies, our own voices are perfectly capable of doing so as well. Simply talking creates sound, and when we communicate with others, we not only communicate through the sound, but the feeling (or "intention") that we put into the sound. The same words uttered in a state of anger, or bliss are still the same words, but they convey a different feeling (or "intention") to the listener. It is therefore important in all meditative healing and invocation techniques to be in a state, or to create a state, of relaxed peace to create the most effective harmonious sound patterns. Making a sound at a natural frequency and holding that sound until it vibrates through the body and visualizing the "intention" of creating health and well-being, can often achieve remarkable results.

There is some debate as to how best to generate and focus these frequencies. There are those that believe that we need a magical formula, intoning sacred sounds and melodies such as are found in the use of mantras and Tibetan chanting. Others believe that simply sounding this single vowel or a short and meaningless word such as "ommmmmmm ..." and holding the note which sets up the strongest waves of oscillation in the body while contemplating and visualizing the "intention", is more effective as it doesn't distract the mind from focusing on its intended purpose.

Jonathan Goldman (*The Lost Chord*: Ethrean 2000) has tried to reproduce what he calls "The Lost Chord". This is defined as the primary sound that initiated creation. As it had the power to create, so too did it have the power to heal and alter thoughts, attitudes, emotions etc. The music is an interesting blend of reverberating chants and sounds that focus on the energy centers of the chakras to awaken energizing them. In his studies he has described how sound can be directed to create physical effects, or as he put it:

Frequency plus intent creates healing.
Vocalization plus visualization creates manifestations.

In his extensive studies, he has highlighted the power of directed sounds produced at the right frequencies as "The Lost Chord".

Sound is therefore a powerful influence in our daily lives and we can potentially harness it for healing, spiritual peace, enlightenment, transcending the physical world connecting with creation and a host of other things besides.

Using Overtone singing techniques described in the book may open the doors into ourselves and help us to achieve that state of harmony with our lives and indeed ourselves that we so often need but we cannot achieve. The trouble with Overtone singing, throat singing, *khoomei*, or whatever name one wishes to call it, is that it is a rigorous and demanding technique that takes a great deal of practice to perform, let alone master. Many of us simply don't have the time or the spare energy to keep trying to achieve what others have developed into a sophisticated art over many generations. So what can we do ourselves?

Well if we can't achieve the heights of *khoomei*, we can still keep trying. It can be surprisingly effective to hum to ourselves quietly, slowly and deliberately, at a note that resonates comfortably with our bodies, or the parts of our bodies that we feel need help. Simply using a chant such as "ommmmmmmmmmm ..." or "amennnnnnnnnnn ...", allowing the final letter to resonate through our bodies as we slowly exhale, going about our business, can do wonders to our physical and psychological states.

Changing the pitch of the vowel or consonant to find the pitch that sends a characteristic tingle through our bodies, is particularly effective, and is quite easy to find and hold when we have found it. Inventing little personal tunes and melodies for yourself as you hum (or "ommm") along is even better!

Playing inspirational, calming, uplifting, or meditative music, depending on our needs, or leaving the hum-drum of the city to sit and listen to the sounds of nature, and even to tune into them by imitating these sounds, (which is how *khoomei* is reputed to have been discovered in the first place) may be better than anything else for maintaining your well-being. Imitating the sounds of a running stream, the wind rustling in the trees, or passing birds, helps to attune us to nature, and its sounds, and helps to promote that sense of well-being and peace that we strive for.

Why not give it a try ... You may well be surprised at how much it does for you!

... whenever I feel afraid,

I whistle a happy tune,
And no one ever knows ... I'm afraid!
Julie Andrews, from the film *The King and I*

'11'

The journey ends

IT HAS BEEN a long, long journey, from East to West , from North to South ... and back again! But this journey hasn't ended, yet, its only beginning!

There is so much information in this book, so much to think about and contemplate, but now is not the time for more words and guidance from a fellow traveller! Now is the time to start exploring yourself, in your own way and in your own time.

May you go in peace and find that elusive something that we're all searching for so desperately!

FURTHER READING

Bloothooft, Gerrit, Eldrid Bringmann, Marieke van Cappellen, Jolanda B van Luipen, and Koen P. Thomassen, "Acoustics and Perception of Overtone Singing". *Journal of the Acoustical Society of America*. vol 4, part 1. October 1992: 1827-1836.

Bregman, Albert S, *Auditory Scene Analysis: The Perceptual Organization of Sound*, Cambridge, Mass.: MIT Press, 1990.

Broadhead, Alex, *Harmonic Singing: An Introduction to the Phenomenon and its Production and Analysis* . Unpublished. Dartmouth College, 1995.

Handel Stephen, *Listening: An Introduction to the Perception of Auditory Events*, Cambridge, Mass.: MIT Press, 1989.

Leet L, *The Secret Doctrine of the Kabbalah: Inner Traditions*, Rochester, New York 1999.

Levin, Theodore, Program notes for "Huur-Huur-Tu: Throat Singers of Tuva". Weigel Hall. Columbus, Ohio. January 1994.

Levin Theodore, *The Hundred Thousand Fools Of God: Musical Travels In Central Asia* (and Queens, New York). Indiana University Press, 1997.

Van Zanten, William and Van Roon, Marjolijn, ed. Oideion. *The Performing Arts World Wide 2*. Research School: Leiden University, 1995.

O

is a symbol of the world,
of oneness and unity. O Books
explores the many paths of wholeness
and spiritual understanding which
different traditions have developed down
the ages. It aims to bring this knowledge
in accessible form, to a general readership,
providing practical spirituality to today's seekers.
For the full list of over 200 titles covering:

- CHILDREN'S PRAYER, NOVELTY AND GIFT BOOKS
  - CHILDREN'S CHRISTIAN AND SPIRITUALITY
    - CHRISTMAS AND EASTER
      - RELIGION/PHILOSOPHY
        - SCHOOL TITLES
          - ANGELS/CHANNELLING
            - HEALING/MEDITATION
              - SELF-HELP/RELATIONSHIPS
                - ASTROLOGY/NUMEROLOGY
                  - SPIRITUAL ENQUIRY
                - CHRISTIANITY, EVANGELICAL
                AND LIBERAL/RADICAL
              - CURRENT AFFAIRS
            - HISTORY/BIOGRAPHY
          - INSPIRATIONAL/DEVOTIONAL
        - WORLD RELIGIONS/INTERFAITH
          - BIOGRAPHY AND FICTION
            - BIBLE AND REFERENCE
              - SCIENCE/PSYCHOLOGY

Please visit our website,
www.O-books.net

SOME RECENT O BOOKS

REIKI MASTERY
For Second Degree Students and Masters
David Vennells

Reiki has many levels and forms, and has changed along the way from the pure, "original" practice of its Buddhist founder, Dr. Mikao Usui. Advanced Reiki, especially above First Degree, is about "facing the mirror," the inner mirror of our own mind. As we progress with our spiritual practice we can begin to clean away the layers of misconception that colour the way we view ourselves, others and the world around us. This is a compassionate, wise, handbook to making the most of the Life Force Energy that surrounds and informs us all.

David Vennells is a Buddhist teacher of Reiki and the author of *Reiki for Beginners, Bach Flower Remedies for Beginners, Reflexology for Beginners.*

1-903816-70-X
£9.99 $14.95

THE THOUGHTFUL GUIDE TO THE BIBLE
Roy Robinson

Most Christians are unaware of the revolution in how the Bible may be understood that has taken place over the last two hundred years. This book seeks to share the fruits of the Biblical revolution in an easily accessible manner. It seeks to inform you of its main features and to encourage you to do your own thinking and come to your own conclusions.

Roy Robinson is a United Reformed Church minister, now retired and living in England. A former missionary in Zaire this work arises from a lifetime of study and Bible teaching at the Oxted Christian Centre, which he founded.

1-903816-75-0
£14.99 $19.95

LET THE STANDING STONES SPEAK
Messages from the Archangels revealed
Natasha Hoffman with Hamilton Hill

The messages encoded in the standing stones of Carnac in Brittany, France, combine and transcend spiritual truths from many disciplines and traditions, even though their builders lived thousands of years before Buddha, Christ and MuhammAd. The revelations received by the authors as they read the stones make up a New Age Bible for today.

"an evergreen..a permanent point of reference for the serious seeker." Ian Graham, author of *God is Never Late*

Natasha Hoffman is a practising artist, healer and intuitive, and lives with her partner Hamilton in Rouziers, France.

1-903816-79-3
£9.99 $14.95

BRINGING GOD BACK TO EARTH
John Hunt

Religion is an essential part of our humanity. We all follow some form of religion, in the original meaning of the word. But organised religion establishes definitions, boundaries and hierarchies which the founders would be amazed by. If we could recover the original teachings and live by them, we could change ourselves and the world for the better. We could bring God back to earth.

"The best modern religious book I have read. A masterwork."
Robert Van de Weyer, author of *A World Religions Bible*

"Answers all the questions you ever wanted to ask about God and
some you never even thought of." Richard Holloway, former
Primus Episcopus and author of *Doubts and Loves*

John Hunt runs a publishing company of which O Books is an
imprint.

1-903816-81-5
£9.99 $14.95

TORN CLOUDS
Judy Hall

Drawing on thirty years experience as a regression therapist and
her own memories and experiences in Egypt, ancient and modern,
Torn Clouds is a remarkable first novel by an internationally-
acclaimed MBS author, one of Britain's leading experts on
reincarnation. It features time-traveller Megan McKennar, whose
past life memories thrust themselves into the present day as she
traces a love affair that transcends time. Haunted by her dreams,
she is driven by forces she cannot understand to take a trip to Egypt
in a quest to understand the cause of her unhappy current life
circumstances. Once there, swooning into a previous existence in
Pharaonic Egypt, she lives again as Meck'an'ar, priestess of the
Goddess Sekhmet, the fearful lion headed deity who was
simultaneously the Goddess of Terror, Magic and Healing.

Caught up in the dark historical secrets of Egypt, Megan is forced
to fight for her soul. She succeeds in breaking the curse that had
been cast upon her in two incarnations.

*Judy Hall is a modern seer who manages the difficult task of evoking
the present world, plus the realm of Ancient Egypt, and making them*

seem real. There is an energy behind the prose, and a power in her imagery which hints that this is more than just a story of character and plot, but an outpouring from another age, a genuine glimpse into beyond-time Mysteries which affect us all today. Alan Richardson, author of *Inner Guide to Egypt.*

Judy Hall has been a karmic counsellor for thirty years. Her books have been translated into over fourteen languages.

1 903816 80 7
£9.99/$14.95

HEALING HANDS
David Vennells

Hand reflexology is one of the most well-known and respected complementary therapies, practised in many hospitals, surgeries, hospices, health and healing centres, and is enjoying a growing popularity. *Healing Hands* explains the simple techniques of Hand Reflexology so clearly, with the aid of illustrations, that "within a few days the reader could be competently treating themselves or others." It is aimed at those interested in learning the practical techniques (how to give yourself and others a full treatment), and also includes the fascinating history of reflexology, how it works with the hands and the various things we can do to support the healing process. As the reader learns the techniques step by step, they can gradually increase their knowledge of anatomy and physiology, together with developing a more accurate awareness of the hand reflexes and how to treat them accurately and successfully.

David Vennells is a Buddhist teacher of Reiki and the author of *Reiki Mastery* (O Books).

1 903816 81 5
£9.99/$16.95

I AM WITH YOU
John Woolley

First published in 1985, and now in its 14th printing, *I Am With You* has been the best-selling devotional in the UK since then. These words of divine encouragement were given to John Woolley in his work as a hospital chaplain, and have since inspired and uplifted tens of thousands, even changed their lives. It is now published for the first time in paperback as an *O Books* title.

I Am With You *will bring peace and consolation to all who read it.* Cardinal Cormac Murphy-O'Connor, Archbishop of Westminster
I commend I Am With You *to all persons who are seeking to deepen their spiritual lives* Cardinal George Basil Hume, former Archbishop of Westminster
A very special book, which will bless countless people Prebendary John Pearce
A lovely book of devotions; we use it daily Dr Donald English, former President Methodist Conference
Wonderfully inspiring Betty Tapscott
A thing of real joy Bishop John Crowley
A most wonderful book which I keep with me always Fr Michael Clothier, O.S.B
The book has changed my life Fr F Bernard, S.J.
The most wonderful book I have read Fr Tom Cass

John Woolley is now retired but continues the work of the *I Am With You Fellowship.*
1 903816 99 8
£6.99/$12.95

HEAD VERSUS HEART-AND OUR GUT REACTIONS
The 21st century enneagram
Michael Hampson

Head versus Heart plots a map of humankind and of the spiritual journeys we take. Based on the enneagram, it is the most important new material on it in thirty years. The enneagram is generally presented as a system of three parts; a list of nine types of people, their arrangement in a circle in a specific order, and their interconnection by a distinctive pattern of internal arrows. Over a hundred books have been published on this material, endlessly describing it, but never explaining it. Most assume ancient Eastern sources as its authority, but none such exist. Into "the gap where the explanation should be" comes the present text.

Written by a highly experienced, wise and practical parish priest, it guides the reader gently and firmly through a whole programme of discovery and-in the proper sense-conversion. This particular reader was forced again and again to recognise the challenging sense of the analysis offered, and hopes that many more will find the same excitement and prompting to growth in these pages. Dr Rowan Williams, Archbishop of Canterbury

Michael Hampson *is an ordained priest of the Church of England, with degrees from Oxford University in Philosophy and Psychology.*

1 903816 92 0
£11.99/$16.95

PSALM
Peter Owen-Jones

The lyrics of the Psalms have survived, being spoken and sung all over the world, because they still communicate the presence of God in all things. Within them are the seeds of understanding, of longing and of being, of being afraid, of being stilled, of being in a state of wonder. But, for many, their language doesn't resonate with contemporary feeling. Once you undo the layers of history and language that have since accumulated you can recover this state of being. Taking its inspiration from rap and country and western this book recasts twelve Psalms in contemporary lyrical genre.

Peter Owen-Jones has been an Anglican priest for ten years and runs four parishes outside Cambridge, England. He is the author of *A Bed of Nails* and *Small Boat, Big Sea*. He recently presented *The Battle for Britain's Soul* on BBC, and his new BBC series comes out in February.

1 903816 91 2
£4.99/$8.95

THE QUEST
Joycelin Dawes

What is your sense of soul? Although we may each understand the word differently, we treasure a sense of who we are, what it is to be alive and awareness of an inner experience and connection with "something more." In *The Quest* you explore this sense of soul through a regular practice based on skills of spiritual reflection and be reviewing the story of your life journey, your encounter with spiritual experience and your efforts to live in a sacred way.

Here you become the teller and explorer of your own story. You can find your own answers. You can deepen your spiritual life through the wisdom and insight of the world's religious traditions. You can revisit the building blocks of your beliefs and face the changes in your life. You can look more deeply at wholeness and connection and make your contribution to finding a new and better way.
So well written, constructed and presented, by a small independent group of individuals with many years experience in personal and spiritual growth, education and community, that it is a joy to work with. It is a life-long companion on the spiritual path and an outstanding achievement; it is a labour of love, created with love to bring more love into our world. Susanna Michaelis, *Caduceus*

1 903816 93 9
£9.99/$16.95